The Battle for Saudia Arabia
Royalty, Fundamentalism, and Global Power

The Battle for Saudia Arabia
Royalty, Fundamentalism, and Global Power

As`ad AbuKhalil

AN OPEN MEDIA BOOK

SEVEN STORIES PRESS • New York

Seven Stories Press
140 Watts Street
New York, NY 10013
www.sevenstories.com

In Canada: Publishers Group Canada, 250A Carlton Street, Toronto, ON M5A-2L1

In the U.K.: Turnaround Publisher Services Ltd., Unit 3, Olympia Trading Estate, Coburg Road, Wood Green, London N22 6TZ

In Australia: Palgrave Macmillan, 627 Chapel Street, South Yarra VIC 3141

ISBN: 1-58322-610-9

9 8 7 6 5 4 3 2 1

College professors may order examination copies of Seven Stories Press titles for a free six-month trial period. To order, visit www.sevenstories.com/textbook/, or fax on school letterhead to (212) 226-1411.

Printed in Canada.

Contents

For all those Saudi men and women who were beheaded or stoned by the executioners of the House of Saud for daring to defy the government's ban on free love.

Author's Note on Transliteration and Translation

In transliterating Arabic, I have diligently followed the old system of the Library of Congress (the one used by Hanna Batatu in his monumental *The Old Social Classes and the Revolutionary Movements of Iraq*). However, for purposes of readability and familiarity, the transliteration had to be simplified (or violated): diacritics could not be used, hence some different Arabic letters had to be Romanized in the same way; diphthongs are not differentiated from vowels. Moreover, for the English pronunciation to be as close as possible to the Arabic, I chose to distinguish between the *shamsi* and the *qamari* letters—for example, "al-Nabi" is spelled "an-Nabi."

Also, in order to avoid confusion and misunderstandings in the mind of the Western reader, names and words that have entered the American (or English) vernacular are used here in the way they have been adopted through popular usage, as inaccurate as such usage may be. For instance, "Sa`ud" is sometimes spelled "Saud," "Yasir `Arafat" is spelled "Yasser Arafat," "Nasir" is spelled "Nasser," and so forth. I have violated some recent American vernacular usages if I believed such usage was way off the original Arabic pronunciation. The word bin or Bin (as in Usamah Bin Ladin) is used in male names in Arabic to refer to the father of the person, as in Usamah Bin (the son of) Ladin. It is also synonymous with

Ibn (and a person may select either). So, for example, the name Khalid bin Sultan implies that Khalid is the son of Sultan. For females it is bint (daughter of).

A.H. refers to the Muslim calendar which began in 622 A.D. when Muhammad and his followers migrated from Mecca to Medina. Unlike the Gregorian calendar, the Muslim calendar is based on a lunar cycle: a 12-month lunar year consisting of 354 or 355 days. Thus, if only given by year, a Muslim calendar date may fall on one of two possible Gregorian calendar years.

Unless otherwise indicated, all translations from Arabic, Persian, and French used in this book are the author's.

To maintain and transmit a value system, human beings are punched, bullied, sent to jail, thrown into concentration camps, cajoled, bribed, made into heroes, encouraged to read newspapers, stood up against the wall and shot, and sometimes even taught sociology. To speak of cultural inertia is to overlook the concrete interests and privileges that are served by indoctrination, education, and the entire complicated process of transmitting culture from one generation to the next.

—Barrington Moore, Jr., *Social Origins of Dictatorship and Democracy: Lord and Peasant in the Making of the Modern World*

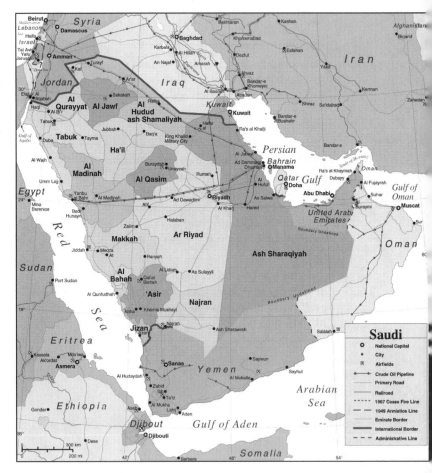

Preface

It was Greg Ruggiero who commissioned me to write this book, and it was Greg who wanted to present to Seven Stories Press readers a critical account of Saudi Arabia and the complex relations that currently exist both within it and between Saudi Arabia and the United States. I wish to express my gratitude and thanks for the careful and thorough editing by Greg, with whom I could disagree only on details but never on substance, and who is able to transform my Arabic-English into English-English. I also want to thank the staff at Seven Stories Press who worked on this book.

In writing this book, I had to draw upon my academic training, and for that I am indebted to Rashid Khalidi of Columbia University—my first political science teacher, from whom I learned a lot. I am glad that Rashid is now carrying the mantle of Edward W. Said. The late Hanna Batatu (of the American University of Beirut and later of Georgetown University) was a great mentor of mine; I admired him a great deal, and missed his insights and perspectives during the recent Bush wars, especially the war on Iraq. Batatu, I am convinced, was deeply wounded by the hypocrisy and cruelty of the 1991 Gulf War. As an early Arab opponent of Saddam, he knew that Western power was in no way interested in the human rights or welfare of the

Iraqi people. In 1984 I saw Batatu give an anti-Saddam talk in Washington, D.C., in his typical soft-spoken but fierce style. The lecture so infuriated Saddam's henchmen (who filled the city during the Reagan-Saddam honeymoon when former diplomat Nizar Hamdoon was the darling of the Washington social and press circles) that they began to take close-up pictures of his face to intimidate him. Batatu, this most gentle human being, was quite frightened and asked my friend Yusuf Al-Khalil and me to escort him to his car. Anyone who wants to learn about Iraq should read Batatu's monumental *The Old Social Classes and the Revolutionary Movements of Iraq* (Princeton University Press, 1978).

Michael Hudson (of Georgetown University) was one of the reasons for my choice of graduate school. He was my adviser and later served as my dissertation adviser and mentor. From Hudson I also learned a great deal and was very impressed with his uniquely critical perspective. He maintained great credibility in his scholarship but did not cater to his audience, whether Western or Middle Eastern. His honesty and integrity serve as a model for all aspiring social scientists.

In the era of social science, one should remain alert to the services of empire, as practiced by New York University's law professor Noah Feldman, who advised the U.S. colonial administrator of Iraq, and who has no qualms about telling Iraqis how they should rule themselves (see his interview on NPR's *Fresh Air*, August 5, 2003), perhaps because he thinks that Westerners are constitutionally endowed. This democratic advocate (as he views himself) has expressed his strong opposition to Iraqi elections because "Iraq is not yet ready" for such a task. (See the text of his Senate testimony at foreign.senate.gov/testimony/2003/FeldmanTestimony030924.pdf). He also objected to democratic elections in Iraq because "the wrong people could get

elected" (*New York Times*, November 29, 2003). He also adds
that "people in the Middle East don't always act rationally"
(*New York Times*, October 7, 2003). Or in the case of a Middle
East anthropologist who is also involved in the U.S. colonial
project in Iraq (on Amal Rassam's role, see *Washington Post*,
November 24, 2003, p. A1), it is important that one offer interpretations and explanations from outside the prism of "embedded" reporters and academics.

In the case of Saudi Arabia, which has a pattern of severe
harassment and repression of its citizens for dissent and frivo-
lous reasons, I refrain from naming any Saudi citizen for fear of
his or her plight. But I can express gratitude nevertheless.
Despite what people may think of Saudis (in the United States
or in the Arab world), there are Saudis who express dissent from
outside the perspective of Islamic fundamentalism. To all the
Saudi Marxists, socialists, feminists, anarchists, and Arab
nationalists that I have met or communicated with over the
years, I offer my thanks. A former U.S. ambassador to the Saudi
kingdom also answered some of my questions on the kingdom
and its royals.

In my last book, many—especially in the Arab world—
expressed astonishment at the very affectionate and loving
words that I expressed toward Maria R. Rosales. People may
not be accustomed to people remaining kind and loving toward
each other after a divorce. So I stand by my effusive words of
admiration and love for Maria, and she, again, went over the
manuscript and tried to make it more readable. I always feel
grateful when I have the opportunity to benefit from her very
brilliant mind and critical eye.

My close friend Julie Weidenfeller has been quite supportive
and interested. Her computer and Internet skills are always
helpful to me, especially in the most stressful and panicky

times. For several years now, Julie has taken time from her innovative computer game designing and testing work to learn about Middle East issues and to be an outstanding friend. Julie has gained more than my affection and friendship. I also wish to mention the many friends, students, and colleagues who improved my thinking either by asking questions, offering insights, showing interest, or even by just being good friends. Specifically, I wish to first thank Neal Christianson, who is one of the most brilliant students I have taught and who kept urging me to start a Web site and would not accept no for an answer. He went ahead and did all the work, despite my objections. My angryarab.blogspot.com owes its creation and continuation to him. Other friends, students, and colleagues that I wish to acknowledge are J. J. Hendricks, Jake Myers, Steven Hughes, Rania AlSweis, Julie Siebens, Emily Gotterich, Nezar AsSayyad, Larry Michalak, Yun Suh, Mayia Shulga, Rhiannon Judd, Valerie Marleau (who went over the proofs to catch typos and errors—and she did so while being sober), `Amer Mohsen, a new Berkeley friend who has offered me advice on matters significant and trivial, Bassam Haddad, Shawna Bader, Rabi` `Aridi (who provided me with tons of Amnesty International documents on the kingdom), Zeina Za`tari, Nadya Sbayti, `Imad Al-Hajj, Joseph Massad, Yogita Maharaj, Emily Barnett, Lisa Agueda, Sinan Antoun, Dimitri Landa, Hanady Salman, Sean Lawson, Amthal Isma`il, Gabriela Doelschner, Lucas Alberto, Mirvat AbuKhalil, Ahmad Dallal, Samah Idriss, Kirsten Scheid Idriss, Maggie Usray, Bronwyn Leebaw, Mona Zaki, Sam Husseini, Holly Welker, Tara Lynn Schendel, Kathy Spillman, Salih Agha, and Marina Throne-Holst. I thank F. Gregory Gause III for sharing with me his writings on Saudi Arabia, and David Barsamian for his interest and encouragement. I also wish to thank my friends at *As-Safir* newspaper in Beirut (Joseph

Samaha, Hanady Salman, and Husan 'Itaani) for providing a free platform for my views and fulminations, and John Zogby of Zogby International, who generously shared with me findings of polls that he'd conducted in the Arab world.

And finally, gratitude to all the folks at KPFA in Berkeley for their deep interest in my work and their promotion of it. And I also want to thank all my students at California State University-Stanislaus, UC-Berkeley, and Colorado College. I have learned from them as they have—I hope—learned from me.

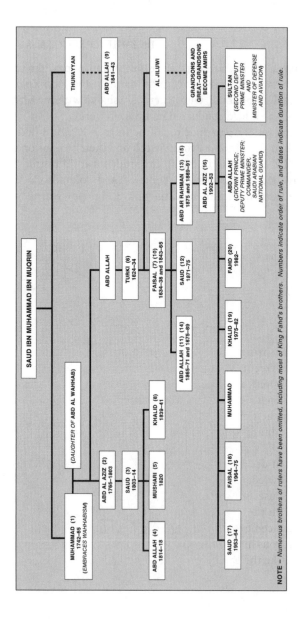

SAUD IBN MUHAMMAD IBN MUQRIN

THUNAYYAN

ABD ALLAH (9)
1841–43

AL JILUWI

GRANDSONS AND
GREAT-GRANDSONS
BECOME AMIRS

MUHAMMAD (1)
1742–55
(EMBRACES WAHHABISM)

(DAUGHTER OF ABD AL WAHHAB)

ABD AL AZIZ (2)
1765–1803

SAUD (3)
1803–14

MUSHARI (5)
1820

KHALID (8)
1839–41

ABD ALLAH (4)
1814–18

ABD ALLAH

TURKI (6)
1824–34

FAISAL (7) (10)
1834–38 and 1843–65

SAUD (12)
1871–75

ABD ALLAH (11) (14)
1865–71 and 1875–89

ABD AR RAHMAN (13) (15)
1875 and 1889–91

ABD AL AZIZ (16)
1902–53

MUHAMMAD

KHALID (19)
1975–82

FAHD (20)
1982–

FAISAL (18)
1964–75

SAUD (17)
1953–64

ABD ALLAH
(CROWN PRINCE;
DEPUTY PRIME MINISTER;
COMMANDER,
SAUDI ARABIAN
NATIONAL GUARD)

SULTAN
(SECOND DEPUTY
PRIME MINISTER
AND
MINISTER OF DEFENSE
AND AVIATION)

NOTE – Numerous brothers of rulers have been omitted, including most of King Fahd's brothers. Numbers indicate order of rule, and dates indicate duration of rule.

Introduction

It is high time for the world to address Saudi Arabia and its bizarre form of government and fanatic ideology. Since at least the 1970s, Saudi oil money has ensured that most, if not all, media in the Arab world be loyal to Saudi royal interests. Thus, Saudi Arabia is either ignored or fawned over in the Arab press. Not that Saudi Arabia's government and royal family have ever been popular in the Arab world. Far from it. But Saudi money has managed to buy off publishers and media owners in order to stifle any manifestation of criticism or even of disagreement with Saudi policies and actions. In the West, the United States leads a decades-long foreign policy that supports Saudi Arabia and protects it from criticism and embarrassment. Oil and other self-serving interests steered previous U.S. administrations away from their hollow slogans about democracy and human rights, including that of Jimmy Carter, the self-described human rights president who never directly acknowledged the Saudi government's corruption, cruelty, and abuse.

Even the U.S. press, which in the aftermath of 9-11 suddenly seemed to discover that there are indeed human rights violations in Saudi Arabia, just as it also suddenly discovered —unlike the European press—that Saddam was a brutal dictator in 1990 after his invasion of Kuwait, has otherwise observed a policy of benign neglect of Saudi human rights violations. Worse, the ambassador of the cruel Saudi regime was treated as a celebrity in the nation's capital, and he was a sought-after guest at fancy parties in Georgetown.

But official U.S. support for the Saudi royal family is not an aberration of U.S. foreign policy. Throughout the decades of the Cold War and long after its end, the United States has disregarded human rights as a principle of foreign policy and only used—and abused—it for political ends. Thus, the story of a Cuban dissident's house being vandalized with graffiti receives attention from the U.S. media (see AP news dispatch December 13, 2003), while stories of dissidents who cannot exist in Saudi Arabia are overlooked and unknown. The result of this systemic bias has been to create the image of the Saudis as "good" Talibans, as opposed to the "bad" Talibans in Afghanistan. Both the Saudis and the Taliban created states governed by fundamentalist religious rule; the Taliban owe their ideological and theological origins to the Saudi Wahhabism. Even the "bad" Taliban in Afghanistan did not bother the U.S. government much prior to September 11. Since World War II, the major criterion for preferential foreign policy from the United States has been the extent to which foreign governments are willing to act subserviently to U.S. political, economic, and military interests, including their willingness to host U.S. troops on their soil. Despite their shared governance through the enforcement of an extreme form of Islamic fundamentalism and a common absence of human rights and democracy, the Saudis have always met U.S. needs and have thus passed the test for friendly treatment in U.S. foreign policy. The Taliban did not.

Saudi Arabia has for years enjoyed excellent relations with

countries in the West and in East Asia. Its oil wealth and purchasing powers gained it strong friendship among the liberal and conservative governments of the world. The 1967 defeat of Egypt, Syria, and Jordan in their war with Israel and the death of Nasser in 1970 removed all hurdles from the Saudi quest for regional supremacy. In the Arab world, this time is often referred to as the dawn of the Saudi Epoch.

But the story of the Saudi economic boom is also a story of cruelty and fanaticism. How could a political system that is based on institutional religious intolerance, misogyny, anti-Shi`ism, and anti-Semitism be indulged for decades? And how could the corrupt rule by the House of Saud go on for such a long time with little scrutiny? And why would Saudi religious fanaticism be permitted to prevail, not only in Arab and Muslim circles but also in Western countries where the royal Sauds have been received as close friends and allies? No oppressive government has received the praise that Saudi Arabia has received since World War II. Even the Soviet Union was kind and generally friendly toward the archconservative royal family.

This book is an attempt to explain to Western readers Saudi Arabia and its ruling ideology—Wahhabiyyah—which speaks in the name of Islam yet deviates from core Islamic notions of tolerance, pragmatism, and moderation. This book is intended for people who have no background in Islamic or Middle Eastern studies, and who wish to educate themselves unfettered by the post–September 11 media biases or the revived Orientalist perspectives that present the Middle East and its people through clichés and stereotypes. The book is based on a large body of published and unpublished literature, and does not rely exclusively on mainstream and official publications. Books on Saudi Arabia in Western libraries are often

Saudi-funded coffee-table books that are PR tools for the royal family. I have read and reread primarily Arabic sources, and others in English and French. As it is essential not to reduce all Saudi opposition to Al-Qa`idah, I have made a special effort to pay close attention to what Saudi opposition groups and dissidents are saying about their country. I have even referred to the literature of Saudi communists in order to remind the reader that oppressive governments—no matter how hard they try—ultimately fail to mold or control the minds of all the citizens. Where there is power, there is opposition, Michel Foucault stressed. And the House of Saud has faced opposition of different stripes from the very beginning of its rule.

I do not wish that my effort here become yet another contribution to the vast literature of hate and hostility toward Arabs and Muslims that has been unleashed since 9-11. The Saudis' oppressive rule, and their Wahhabiyyah state doctrine are very minor aspects of life in the Middle East, and the Saudi people have selected neither by their own free will. Both have been imposed on them, first by swords and later by fighter jets supported by powerful backers: the British and, later, the Americans. If anything, the Saudi people have tried on many occasions to express their opposition to the royal government but have been brutally suppressed. Unfortunately, some of the opposition has been expressed through equal or parallel fanaticism, which is exemplified by the Al-Qa`idah movement and its ilk. But such movements are logical extensions, or outgrowths, of Saudi indoctrination or oppression, or both.

This book does not focus, as others frequently have, on the travails of the royal family and its princes. To be sure, attention is paid to this quixotic group of princes, but it also devotes a section to the unheard voices of Saudi subjects: to the women and dissidents of the kingdom whose profiles are kept out of Western newspapers due to Saudi financial power and lobbying influence. The book also pays attention to the "firm bond" that binds Saudi Arabia to successive American administrations, including those who have preached human rights and democracy, betraying their hollow rhetoric, which has been met with derision and mockery in the Middle East. The people there have become familiar with the marriage of the House of Saud and the House of Uncle Sam.

I strongly believe that Saudi Arabia has caused a lot of damage to the region and its important causes. It certainly succeeded in fighting a promising movement that emerged from the left, and it has opposed all vestiges of "Western" enlightenment (rationality, scientific research, secularism, and skepticism) and progress. Instead, the enormous financial power of the Saudi family has been utilized to spread fundamentalist messages of exclusiveness, intolerance, puritanism, misogyny, and traditionalism. It has also marketed and helped project European colonialism and, later, American domination in the region. And with its financial power, the government succeeded in silencing its critics (especially in the Arab world)—sometimes by killing them, as was allegedly the case with Nasir As-Sa`id—and salarying a pliant Arab press, including those Arabic publications that are published in London, ostensibly away from Arab censors. In the age of satellite television, the Saudi royals are also moving fast to establish their hegemony through buyouts, mergers, massive briberies, and monopolies.

Saudi Arabia, as will be seen here, is a country that defies reform or modification. It is a government that should be overthrown; a brutal dictatorship wed to an ideology of religious fanaticism should not be allowed to continue in this century. This, however, should not be interpreted as an invi-

tation for yet another American "war of liberation."
Emancipation is possible—or is only possible—without U.S.
bombs and bullets. People of the Middle East have become
too accustomed to regime change engineered by Washington,
starting from as early as 1949 in Syria, when the CIA imposed
military dictator Husni Az-Za`im. The people of the Middle
East have never been impressed with America's chosen representatives. The United States usually replaces an anti-
American dictator with a pro-American dictator. For example,
the current governing council of Iraq is a puppet mélange of
embezzlers, unknowns, fundamentalists, and former henchmen of Saddam's regime. The change in Saudi Arabia should
come from within.

The world community, however, should play a helping role
in isolating the royal family and in assisting the voices of
change and progress in the dark kingdom. And the U.S. government should not express concern about a country's human
rights record only as leverage to extract more political and
economic concessions from that country. Libya's dictator,
Mu`ammar Al-Qadhdhafi, knows this all too well. In late 2003
he announced a unilateral abandonment of Libya's programs
to produce chemical, biological, and nuclear weapons. Once
he made the announcement, his human rights violations and
his oblique admission of Libya's responsibility for the bombing of Pan Am Flight 103 seemed to all but vanish. The White
House began referring to him in respectful terms; seemingly
overnight, the once rogue Libyan dictator suddenly became
Colonel Qadhdhafi. The connections between Saudi Arabia,
Wahhabiyyah, and the United States need to be discussed in
blunt language and without fear of antagonizing the royal sensibilities of the Saudi rulers, the fundamentalist sensibilities
of the Saudi clerical establishment, or the hegemonic sensibil-

ities of the U.S. government. The people of Saudi Arabia deserve—as do all people—to have their story told without deference to their oppressors.

ONE

The Paradoxes of Saudi Arabia

On the night of September 11, 2001, the powerful Saudi ambassador to the United States, Prince Bandar Bin Sultan, received a phone call from CIA director George Tenet informing him that fifteen of the nineteen hijackers were citizens of the kingdom. He, as he recounts the story, did not believe the news at first; in fact, his uncle, Prince Nayif, the minister of the interior, continued for months to deny that fifteen of the hijackers came from Saudi Arabia. The news was too damaging for the royal family, who had enjoyed unusually close relations with successive U.S. administrations. Whether Democrat or Republican, American presidents have always protected the interests of the kingdom in the United States and have shielded the royal family from Congress and the press. After 9-11, that began to change. Not that George W. Bush has been unprotective of the Saudi royal family. He has. But press, public, and congressional criticisms of the kingdom have gotten to be louder and wider. The Bush administration has not stopped its efforts to improve the image of the royal family, but those efforts are now more arduous. You see, they deal with a special kind of royal and a special kind of government.

Saudi Arabia is an unusual country. It is home both to fabulous oil wealth and Islam's two holiest sites. Saudi Arabia is one of the world's most oppressive and misogynistic countries, but it enjoys an international status that ignores its long record of what Amnesty International has called "continuing gross human rights violations."[1] A country that imports the latest modern technology and weaponry, it still refuses to respond to rising demands for political participation, clinging to a mode of government derived from medieval practices and extreme theological interpretations. Today, in the year 2004, the kingdom of Saudi Arabia poses a challenge to the international system. As the United States invaded Iraq in the name of liberating its people from tyranny, the Bush administration along with international powers continued to respect, praise, and support the Saudi government, which is itself arguably tyrannical. How could an oppressive royal family with a strict attachment to an obscurantist ideology maintain excellent ties with Western democracies that pride themselves on their adherence to liberal democratic principles? The most glaring paradox regarding Saudi Arabia is its close alliance with the United States, the country that packages its violent campaigns around the world as part of a fight for democracy and human rights.

THE U.S.-SAUDI PARADOX

Until September 11, 2001, the United States and Saudi Arabia had enjoyed an unusually close relationship. The U.S. had dealt with the Saudis with a peculiar respect that they did not usually extend to other countries with as embarrassing human rights records. Unfortunately, this is not to say that U.S. support for the oppressive Saudi government is inconsistent with the record of U.S. foreign policy. Even so, the

medieval nature of the Saudi system and its imposition of a
fanatical state religion should have raised some alarm, at
least in liberal circles. Even Jimmy Carter, who spoke—and
only spoke—openly about human rights during his administration, continued along the previously established path of
American endorsement of the Saudi royal family. After the
Soviet invasion of Afghanistan in 1979, which Carter said
taught him about communism, he reestablished and consolidated a strategic alliance with Saudi Arabia. This powerful
alliance would later help spawn the global Islamic fundamentalist movement, represented by the likes of Bin Ladin. In
the aftermath of 9-11, even when a substantial segment of
the American population felt that Saudi Arabia was in some
regard an enemy, Washington continued to praise the Saudi
royals. According to a public opinion survey published in
2002, neutral to very negative American views of Saudi
Arabia increased from 63 percent in 1994 to a whopping 81
percent in 2002.[2] Despite public opinion, the official relationship between the two governments continued to grow
and prosper. When press reports contained many critical stories of Saudi Arabia in the wake of September 11, the U.S.
government dissociated itself from those reports and declared
its friendship with the royal family. In 2002 George W. Bush
telephoned the crown prince of Saudi Arabia to "reassure him
of the countries' 'eternal friendship.'"[3] The phrase "eternal
friendship" has no standing in international law or global
diplomacy, and its meaning was not subsequently clarified
by the White House. Nevertheless, the statement clearly signals that, despite 9-11 and the global "war on terrorism," the
United States plans to maintain perpetual and continuous
support for the Saudi system in return for the military, economic, and political services that they have undertaken, and

continue to undertake, on behalf of U.S. interests. The commitment is at the heart of the U.S.–Saudi paradox, as it runs contrary to the American public's perception that U.S. foreign policy is implacably rooted in the advance of democracy, human rights, and freedom, none of which, by American definitions, currently exist in Saudi Arabia.

The paradoxical relationship between Saudi Arabia and the United States began with that famous meeting between Franklin D. Roosevelt and Ibn Saud (known as King `Abdul-`Aziz in Arabic). But the relationship is paradoxical when analyzed from the standpoint of the anticommunist obsession that drove the foreign policies of both nations. The reactionary religious ideology of the House of Saud was quite appealing for American policy makers during the Cold War, especially when progressive and secular ideologies were sweeping the Middle East. It was then, and not during the 1980s as is commonly assumed, that the strategic alliance between the United States and Saudi Arabia was first inaugurated. It was cemented during the Reagan years (although it was strong during the Carter years as well) when CIA director William Casey was looking for ways to fund his worldwide adventures and to circumvent a congressional ban on U.S. funding for the Nicaraguan contras.[4] The aggressive and ambitious Saudi ambassador to the United States, Prince Bandar Bin Sultan, was hoping to elevate the U.S.–Saudi relations beyond the oil-and-arms relationship into a strong and stable strategic alliance. As part of this plan, King Fahd, through Prince Bandar, helped fund U.S. efforts in the Middle East during the 1980s.[5] That the relationship improved and progressed should not be surprising; the United States has had many antidemocratic allies besides Saudi Arabia, as exemplified by a close and supportive relationship with

Saddam Husayn's Iraq.[6] On the other hand, there is a peculiarity to the Saudi political and religious system which the United States has had to ignore in order to maintain the relationship and to rationalize arms sales to the country. The United States has often had to invoke the "noninterference in internal affairs" of other countries slogan in order to excuse its failure to hold Saudi Arabia accountable to any human rights standard. The slogan became hard to swallow after the 1991 Gulf War, as the world became accustomed to American dispatch of troops to reverse events, impose imperial will, and, since at least 9-11, to change regimes.

Without a doubt, the relationship between the two countries has become more complex and tense since September 11. The American public has not overcome the fact that fifteen of the nineteen hijackers came from Saudi Arabia. Many Saudi royals were convinced that Al-Qa`idah strategically selected Saudi hijackers in order to create a rift between the United States and the royal family, although there is no evidence that such a rift has occurred. Yet as far as the press, the public, and large sectors of Congress were concerned, the post–9-11 climate and the many acts of violence, occupation, detention, and war that have been waged in the name of fighting terrorism have all made Saudi Arabia an unattractive ally of the American people. The Bush administration, however, continuing in the tradition of previous administrations, never wavered in its support for Saudi-American relations. The Saudi royal family has tried its best to control the spin on Saudi involvement in the crisis; envoys were sent, and the national security advisor of Crown Prince Abdullah, `Adil Al-Jubayr, set up shop in Washington, D.C., an angry city looking for answers in the aftermath of the September 11 attacks.

The royal family entered a crisis zone after September 11—a zone defined by several potent forces. The first is the Arab world's rage against the United States for invading and occupying two Islamic countries, and for Washington's unwavering support for Israel throughout its brutal occupation and collective punishment of the Palestinian people. The second force is the increasing pressure to deliver on Washington's demands to comply with its war on terrorism, aspects of which—especially the financial and curricular components—clash with the very basis of legitimacy of the Saudi state. For example, how can the Saudi government investigate and crack down on the numerous philanthropic institutions inside and outside the kingdom when *zakat* (almsgiving) constitutes one of the five pillars of the Islamic faith? How can the Saudi government crack down on charities that primarily alleviate Palestinian suffering without appearing to be in the service of the Israelis' cause? How could the Saudi state "reform its educational system" without diluting Wahhabi doctrine, which constitutes a founding element of its religio-political legitimacy? And yet, complicating matters further is the third potent force defining the Saudi royals' dilemma: the very real presence of extremist networks inside Saudi Arabia that have struck with increasing sophistication and ruthlessness since the May 2003 bombings in residential Riyadh.

The crisis in Saudi-American relations intensified in July 2003 when the U.S. Congress issued a September 11 investigation report that, according to press accounts, contained scathing condemnation of the Saudi government and stated that members of the ruling family were complicit in terrorism.[7] The Saudi government sent the foreign minister to help ease the tensions, but he returned to Saudi Arabia even more convinced of an anti-Saudi campaign in Washington, D.C. In August 2003 Prince

Saud Al-Faysal accused Congress of not listening to Saudi concerns and was critical of the U.S. war on terrorism.[8] Yet the Saudi government insists on maintaining its ties to the American government for fear of losing the close military arrangement that keeps the royal family securely in power in a turbulent region where they have very few admirers, except either those who are on its payroll or those of its subjects whose support is the safest form of opposition against the increasing influence of fanatical Wahhabi fundamentalism.

Because of this—though the president has seldom been more than mildly critical, and even then only behind the scenes and through anonymous officials—the Saudi government never tires in its desperate attempts to please a skeptical U.S. Congress. In August 2003 the Saudi government and the United States secretively agreed that the FBI and IRS would be able to investigate terrorist links and operate freely on Saudi soil.[9] In an attempt to satisfy those in Congress who keep calling for curricular reforms and reduction in state-supported religious instruction, the Saudi government announced that it would introduce English language instruction at the primary level as of the following school year.[10] It is doubtful that either the American critics would be appeased or that Saudi royal troubles would end soon.

THE ARAB PARADOX

The Saudi royal family has been derided in Arab popular culture and literature for decades. Despite being the host of the Muslim world's two holiest sites, its brand of Islam—Wahhabism—strikes most Muslims as fanatical and eccentric at best. Jamal `Abdul-Nasser (the popular Egyptian leader who ruled from 1952 to1970) made a career of mocking the House of Saud. His attacks on the royal family, and on the oil-rich Gulf rulers in general, characterized Arab political discourse for much of the 1950s and 1960s. This was the era that Malcolm Kerr characterized as the Arab Cold War.[11] Nasser's attacks on King Faysal in the 1960s bore fruit; he succeeded in instigating the first-ever defection from the royal family. A brother of the king, Prince Talal Bin `Abdul-`Aziz (father of famous billionaire Prince Al-Walid Bin Talal), fled to Egypt and announced the creation of the Free Princes movement in 1962.[12] The movement adopted Nasser's slogans of Arab nationalism and anti-Westernism. It later disintegrated and Prince Talal was allowed back into the kingdom, though he was reportedly barred for life from holding any ministerial position (sons of the kingdom's `Abdul-`Aziz Ibn Saud, known in the West as Ibn Saud, are guaranteed ministerial positions).

Though Nasser's anti-Saudi propaganda was popular and somewhat effective, when the news of Israel's 1967 victory over the Arabs was revealed, Nasser almost completely stopped his anti-Saudi line. He needed Saudi financial support to rebuild Egyptian armed forces and therefore became unable and unwilling to attack the Saudi government. The death of Nasser removed the last stumbling block on the path of Saudi propaganda in the Arab world. A new era, the Saudi Epoch (al-hiqbah as-Sa`udiyyah), spread its wings throughout the region. Petrodollars dominated the media. With the exception of those under the influence of generous subsidies and gifts from the regime of Saddam Husayn, Arab media were under Saudi control. Even the PLO was easy to control through direct funding of its major groups—through the mainstream Fatah (more accuarately, Fath) movement and through a relationship between the royal family and the politically shifty

Yasser `Arafat. The Saudi ability to control the political and media culture of the region also coincided with Saudi dominance within the League of Arab States (the regional organization that comprises all Arab countries and the Palestinian authority). Saudi Arabia's fellow Arab countries had been easy to shape and mold with promises of financial aid and access to royal largesse.

All this facilitated the stifling of debate over Saudi affairs. Nevertheless, detestation of Saudi practices and policies remained under the surface. Some brave writers, such as `Abdul-Muhsin Musallam, expressed themselves against Saudi royal excesses and were either arrested or banned from the kingdom altogether. (Musallam's poem addressed the corrupt judges in the kingdom by saying: "Your beards are smeared with blood. You indulge a thousand tyrants and only the tyrant do you obey").[13] One of the most critically acclaimed Arab novelists, `Abdur-Rahman Munif, was stripped of his citizenship and banned from the kingdom. (And when Munif died in January 2004, the royal family tried to coopt his family by offering financial rewards and perks. The family refused and insisted on their right to attain citizenship. The government refused, after bragging in the Saudi press about its "generous offer."[14]) The same fate met the Syrian poet Nezar Qabbani, who ridiculed the lifestyles of Saudi princes and resented the impact of oil on Arab life and politics (although this Qabbani was enamored of Saddam Husayn and specialized in sexist—ostensibly erotic—poetry):

> Oil is lying down happy under the trees of drowsi-
>   ness; and between the breasts of *Harem*;
> This which has visited us, clothed as the stonable
>   Satan;

Oil, this semen; it is not nationalist, nor Arab, nor
    popular;
This rabbit that gets defeated in all wars;
It is a beverage for great emperors; it is not a bever-
    age of the people.[15]

But if the Saudi royal family could not control the free-
thinkers or the consciousness of the people, it easily controlled
the governments and the pliant Arab press. After the 1991 Gulf
War and the demise of the financial power of Saddam's regime,
the Saudi government dispatched its present-day deputy minister of defense, Khalid Bin Sultan (son of the minister of
defense and half-brother of Prince Bandar Bin Sultan, Saudi
ambassador in Washington, D.C.), to ensure Saudi financial
and political control of the Arab press. Even the previously
staunchly pro-Saddam publications, like the Paris-based *Al-
Watan Al-`Arabi*, turned pro-Saudi overnight. Owners of the
influential *Al-Hayat* newspaper would not sell the paper, so a
hefty sum was paid to lease it.[16] With the demise of Saddam's
power, the Saudi government had the Arab scene, at least the
official Arab scene, all to themselves.

But herein lies the paradox. How could such a despised and
defiled government control so much of the region's press?
How could the scandals of the Saudi royal family be kept out
of all the Arab newspapers? And how could the small and
extremist Wahhabiyyah sect of Saudi Arabia stifle religious
debate in the entire region and prevent critical examination of
a doctrine that is at variance with mainstream Islamic beliefs?
For that to occur, of course, Saudi Arabia had to encourage a
climate of intimidation and autocracy. Transparency and
accountability run counter to Saudi political and religious
interests. The Arab paradox of Saudi Arabia, that a despised

government nevertheless became the primary voice the world heard from the Arab region, may not last much longer. Non-Saudi-funded Arab satellite news media—like Al-Jazeera—are opening up avenues of uncensored information, opinion, and debate. Moreover, the rise of the Bin Ladin phenomenon also exposed, both within and outside the Arab world, the embarrassing realities behind Saudi claims. After 9-11, the family could no longer insist on favorable press coverage.

THE SAUDI PARADOX

It is perhaps no longer possible for the Saudi political formula to endure. The kingdom of Saudi Arabia was founded in 1932 on the basis of a marriage of convenience between the House of Shaykh and the House of Saud. This connection was established to cement the relationship between the country's two-wings of ruling elite. The House of Shaykh represents the kingdom's clerical establishment and takes care of Wahhabiyyah indoctrination and propagation, while the House of Saud rules politically so long as it upholds Wahhabism's fundamentalist Islamic norms. Yet, through the state and its agencies, the House of Shaykh promotes the most puritanical, exclusivist, and intolerant version of Islam, while members of the royal family live ostentatious and hedonistic lives that contradict the state's most basic precepts. How can the state continue to maintain its legitimacy when the governing family embodies a flagrant and perpetual violation of the core rules and beliefs propagated by official state schools and mosques and enforced by religious police? This question, in essence, triggered the 1979 rebellion inside the holy mosque of Mecca in which a religious student named Juhayman Ibn Muhammad Al-`Utaybi took the teachings of Wahhabiyyah and used them to judge the House of Saud. The movement that rose out of his criticisms was brutally crushed and he was summarily executed. While Bin Ladin is not a graduate of formal religious institutions (contrary to press reports, he is neither a cleric nor an engineer; he has a degree in public administration and management), he can be seen as another example of the opposition to the hypocrisy of royal rule—opposition derived from the perspective of official state policy, Wahhabi Islam. Every Saudi, whether he or she wants it or not, is compelled to receive a high dosage of religious indoctrination at all levels of education, through the state-owned media which still observe the times of prayer five times a day, and through roving religious police that enforce the rules in the streets and public places.

These forces, in addition to American demands for "democratic" changes and the stemming of Wahhabiyyah influence, will inevitably produce a conflict in the body of the ruling establishment. This conflict will most likely constitute the crisis that eats through the bond between the House of Shaykh and the House of Saud and brings down the House of Saud's reign.

At the same time that the royals are managing simmering internal pressures, they are constantly managing intense American demands and dictates, and they have been acting accordingly. An advisor to the crown prince bragged to reporters in August 2003 that the kingdom had adopted a series of "reforms," including the prevention of money transfer by philanthropic organizations without government permission; the supervision of the accounts of some 245 charities; the freezing of "some" assets and the closure of 12 branches of charitable foundations; the ouster of 700 "hard-line" clerics; and the ban on 1,500 preachers who can no longer offer sermons or issue fatwas.[17] It is unlikely that those changes will satisfy either Washington, D.C., or followers of the Saudi Wahhabiyyah movement, who are repulsed by the heavy-handed influence of the U.S. government.

ORIENTALIST PARADOX

The Orientalist paradox is important for understanding some of the blind biases that skew academic study and critique of Saudi Arabia. Orientalism refers here to the body of Western academic knowledge and study of the Middle East. Edward W. Said's landmark book *Orientalism* also reminds us that Orientalism is more than a system of knowledge and study; it is a mode of control. Orientalism is the product of an ignorant system that promotes epistemological—and in some cases genetic—distinctions between Western people (who are supposed to be rational, humane, and advanced) and Eastern people, who remain hostages to backwardness, irrationality, and barbarism. Its biases characterized the Western colonization of the region, and the ideological arsenal of Western colonization remains in play now, during the age of U.S. empire. The same clichés and stereotypes about Arabs and Muslims that one read in eighteenth- and nineteenth-century works and travelers' accounts are now widely read in U.S. newspapers and officials' speeches in Washington, D.C.

There is no question that Saudi Arabia arouses the interest of Western media and academia. To most in the United States and elsewhere in the West, Saudi Arabia's political system and fundamentalist ideology seem bizarre and extreme, and thus only reinforce the sense of the exotic that has long attracted Orientalist interests. That there are more biographies of Bin

Ladin and Abu Nidal in the West than there are of Arab artists, architects, and thinkers demonstrates Western fixation with the violent and fanatical. The Orientalist paradox is that such writings claim concern for the plight of human rights in Saudi Arabia, yet many Western writings (especially in popular culture) about Saudi Arabia reek with ignorance and contempt for Saudi people. The best example is perhaps Sandra Mackey. She is not a trained scholar of the Middle East, nor does she know any of its languages. Yet she has become, since the publication of her book *The Saudis*, an authority on the Middle East and has been appointed an in-house expert at CNN. Mackey lived in Saudi Arabia with her physician husband and wrote anonymous articles for a Western readership before she left the kingdom and wrote her book.[18] *The Saudis* became an instant best seller after the Gulf War triggered mass interest in the Middle East. Mackey's book includes tales of Saudi men and women making love with their clothes on,[19] of Saudi women eating and drooling,[20] of Saudi people restocking food during Ramadan like "nocturnal animals,"[21] and she asserts that "science has failed to penetrate the minds of Saudi males."[22]

Another such "expert" is Robert Lacey, who has, since the publication of his book on the kingdom, become something of an accepted authority on Saudi Arabia and the Arabs. He has this to say: "Arab fatalism is a racial as well as a religious characteristic. It contains a strong element of incuriosity— plain intellectual idleness—and it also involves a certain amount of arrogance and 'face.'"[23] Another example is an American journalist who wrote a book on the kingdom and who, in addition to making multitudes of generalizations, states: "Saudi radio is so bad, it is not worth discussing."[24] Most recently a right-wing ideologue who knew how to appeal to the fears of the American people produced a book on Islam and Wahhabiyyah. In it, he assures us that the Saudi royal family "reproduced the structure of Bolshevism and Nazism."[25] This is some of what passes as Western authoritative knowledge on the Middle East.

When applied to Saudi Arabia, all too often everything is permitted, no matter how prejudiced and ill informed. Perhaps because Saudi Arabia is a self-declared Muslim nation, this allows non-Muslim Western writers to interpret all phenomena in the kingdom as expressions of Islam, an approach that is too often a staple of Western scholarship and culture with regard to the Middle East. Such ignorance cannot be dismissed because it determines the bulk of Middle East knowledge in U.S. culture. In addition to biased academics and journalists, Saudi Arabia has also been seen and interpreted through hired lobbyists or political propagandists. The next chapter will present the country as it is, through a definition and presentation of Saudi Arabia.

TWO

What Is Saudi Arabia?

NAME AND PEOPLE

It is important to note that Saudi Arabia was not created naturally as a result of an internal process of tribal consolidation but out of an alliance between one colonial power, Britain, and one tribe, the House of Saud. This alliance became viable only due to outside sponsorship by the United Kingdom, sponsorship that was later replaced by the United States. Today Saudi Arabia is recognized by the UN and is a member of the League of Arab States. Yet before its creation by colonial powers, Saudi Arabia did not exist in distinct geographical or political terms.

This of course is not unique to Saudi Arabia; many countries of the region have been produced as a result of colonial manipulations and indigenous tribal machinations, and borders were often constructed by the fountain pens of colonial officers. But Saudi Arabia is unique in that it is named after the man who founded the country—Al Saud and his descendant family. In Arabic, the full name of the country translates as the Saudi Arab kingdom; in English the country is more commonly known simply as Saudi Arabia. The designation of "Saudi Arabia" is meant to distinguish this part of Arabia from the rest, which leads us to the notion of Arabia.

Arabia is one of those Western names given to a region to simplify geography for Western audiences and armies. There is no exact Arabic counterpart for Arabia; it was historically known as the Peninsula of the Arab (*Jazirat Al-`Arab*). The ancient Greeks coined the term "Arabia" and derived the name from those pastoral people known as "the Arabs."[26] The name initially was applied to the northern areas of the peninsula, and later to the whole of it. The Romans recognized the distinction between Arabia Deserta and Arabia Felix, although the distinction was not scientific and presumably they did not have sufficient geographic knowledge to identify the "rocky" versus the "fertile" parts of the terrain.

Arabia is bigger than India, and deserts occupy large portions of its terrain, although some fertile parts of it defy the term Arabia Deserta. When the peninsula was traversed by camel in 1923, it took forty-seven days: twenty-four days from Kuwait to Riyadh and twenty-three days from Riyadh to Mecca.[27] Some parts of Arabia were distinct (at least in names and historical memories) long before the advent of the borders and administrative divisions of the twentieth century. Al-Hijaz referred to the northern and western parts, which house the Muslim holy sites in Mecca and Medina. (Medina, or Medinat an-Nabai— the City of the Prophet, literally, was known as Yathrib before the migration of the Prophet from Mecca to Medina in 622, which marked the beginning of the Muslim calendar). `Asir denotes the western part of Arabia, south of Hijaz and north of Yemen. It is more fertile than other parts of the region. But Najd is the main section of Arabia, and it denotes the central Arabian desert of the peninsula. Al-Ihsa', or Al-Hasa, refers to the western coast of the Persian Gulf and the eastern part of Saudi Arabia, where the majority of the country's Shi`ite population lives. It is also the region containing the most oil.

The emergence of Islam left an indelible mark on the peninsula, which absorbed the culture and influences of the new faith, along with the great population movements that it inspired. Of course, the peninsula was never an isolated place (although it contained isolated places that did not see vegetation or rain); it was located "at one of the principal junctures of trade routes in the world—between the basin of the Indian Ocean and its Asian extensions in the 'East,' and the basin of the Mediterranean Sea and its African and European extensions in the 'West.'"[28] The eastern seaports had been active in trade with India, East Africa, Persia, and Mesopotamia. The western ports, on the other side, were active in trade with the Mediterranean through the Red Sea. By land, Arabia hosted caravan trades from southern Arabia to the northern parts of Arabia and ultimately to Persia, Egypt, Syria, and Mesopotamia. There was pilgrimage trade and commerce in Mecca before Islam, as Mecca was a center of pagan worship. Muhammad, once victorious against the pagan factions of Mecca, destroyed idol worship and did not prevent pilgrimage altogether but reversed its purpose. Instead of paying homage to the gods and goddesses of pre-Islamic Arabia, Islam now commanded that a Muslim perform pilgrimage "at least once in a lifetime" to Mecca, to pay homage to Allah, and only to Allah. Up until the discovery of oil, hajj (pilgrimage to Mecca)—one of the five pillars of Islam—constituted a major revenue stream for the nascent kingdom.

Since the seventh century, Arabia has been closely associated with Islam and its prophet, Muhammad. Muhammad was born in Mecca in 569. In 622, under pressure from elders of his own tribe, he was forced to migrate to Medina. The two cities became the holiest sites in the Islamic world, and the Al-Hijaz region that contained both cities attained a measure of holiness that would be crucial for the political legitimacy of whoever ruled the area. But the political significance of Arabia for Islam did not last long. For geopolitical reasons, within a few decades of the death of Muhammad, Islam's center of political gravity shifted away from Arabia to Damascus, and later to what is today Iraq. Islamic caliphates sprouted in various parts of the Muslim world but not in Arabia. Arabia's political decline continued over the centuries, although the holy sites of Islam continued to attract millions of pilgrims from around the world.

The indigenous people of Saudi Arabia have been associated with nomadic Bedouin lifestyles. Amazingly, today almost one of every ten people living in the kingdom remain nomadic. Even in Muhammad's lifetime, large numbers of Arabians were city people and therefore not constantly moving in search of shelter and vegetation. Without reducing the culture to stereotypes, one can say that many old Bedouin cultural influences remain today: macho—typically sexist—concepts of manhood; great emphasis on hospitality, tribal alliances and conflicts, generosity, falconry, hunting, respect for elders, and a certain fatalism.[29] However, these values do not on their own shape the popular and cultural outlooks of the people of the region, since many other value systems have also penetrated the social and cultural mores. Regarding prudishness, for example, what passes in Saudi Arabia today as sexual mores is nothing but imported Victorian values. Early Islam was sexually permissive and explicit to a degree that scandalized and horrified Western Christians. Of course, classical Orientalists and their ideological descendants tend to stress either Islam or nomadic culture, or both, to the exclusion of other influential forces. Raphael Patai, in his notorious *The Arab Mind* (which witnessed a resurgence in sales and editions after September 11), constructs his case on the assumption that all Arabs still live nomadically.[30]

The very project of state formation was fundamentally alien to the continuation and freedom of Bedouin lifestyles. As the neoconservative Lebanese sociologist Waddah Shararah observes, "The firm, unitary, and total leadership carries within it the death of Bedouin society: peace undermines Bedouin lifestyle..."[31] Moreover, there are in the nomadic lifestyles inherent streaks of rebelliousness, antiauthoritarianism, and opposition to centralization and private property. The state was the enemy of nomads, and states, including Saudi Arabia, had to launch wars to subdue them. To this day, the Israeli state fights against Arab Bedouins who resist state encroachments on their lands and lifestyles.

TRIBES

The Bush administration's post–9-11 invasions and occupations of Afghanistan and Iraq have heightened the political salience of tribe. But there is no unified meaning of "tribe." "The word is used to refer to kinship group, an extended family, or a coalition of related families."[32] Albert Hourani did not think that tribe should be understood in terms of kinship but more in terms of an imagined common ancestry, very much along the lines of Benedict Anderson's definition of nations as "imagined communities."[33] The formation of the Saudi state has been closely related to tribes and tribal associations, which should not be understood in themselves but as an expression of regional alliances and extensions of colonial rules and policies. Thus, the Ottomans aligned themselves with Ibn Rashid and the British with As-Subah,

As-Sa`ud, the Idrisi of `Asir, and the Hashemites of Hijaz. Alliances translated into subsidies, arms, and favored status when possible.[34]

Early in the twentieth century, Saudi society was tribally structured; a majority of the people living in the areas of Najd, Al-Qasim, and Al-Ahsa' were nomadic.[35] The tribe provided the individual with social and political identity, security (physical and emotional), a moral economy of collective welfare, and a willing and ready army for self-defense or raids. Tribal leadership recognized age; maleness; and a reputation for fairness, courage, wisdom, and qualities of machismo—assertiveness and bluntness (*muru'ah* in classical Arabic captures the meaning of those "virtues"). A tribal leader and council govern a tribe; these practices are not antiquated in present-day Saudi Arabia, as they are incorporated into Saudi royal political practices. However, this should not be exaggerated, as it was by *Los Angeles Times* reporter David Lamb when he dubbed those practices "desert democracy."[36] To a greater degree than the tribal council, the "traffic" between public and royalty is subject to standards of wealth, power, prestige, and blood, and has been severely restricted since the assassination of King Faysal in 1975 by his nephew. There is, however, a system of reception of grievances at the local level, depending on the personality and disposition of individual princes. Prince Salman, governor of Riyadh, for example, has a reputation of openness and accessibility and is a royal aspirant himself.

Saudis manipulated some tribes (like `Utaybah, Subay`, and Mutayr) and fought others (like the Hashemites and the Shammar). To solidify his rule (and perhaps to satisfiy his appetite), founding King `Abdul-`Aziz (known in the West as Ibn Sa`ud) married into many other tribes and families, and he left not only thirty-nine sons but many (politically irrelevant—

by the standards of the House of Saud) daughters as well. State formation and modernization caused a major shift in tribal location and structure. First, state land aggrandizement abolished the exclusive tribal entitlement in a grazing zone.[37] Second, the Saudi state identity, in addition to the nascent Arab national identity in its heyday, posed a serious challenge to the monopoly of social and political identity that had long been enjoyed by tribes. This did not necessarily eliminate tribal identities, but it added layers of identity that may not have existed before. Third, the tribes had to find avenues within the state to advance their own welfare and status: either by intermarriage with As-Sa`ud or through integration with the tribally structured National Guard. This National Guard was intended to bring tribes into the state and to create a loyal internal force. Fourth, some tribes were favored over others: the favored tribes were given large parcels of land, which made their tribal chieftains into large landowners. Fifth, tribal values influenced the state value system as long as they conformed to Wahhabi ideology, the state ideology. The deep socioeconomic inequalities that have been introduced and intensified by oil wealth, and by the unfair policies of the royal families, generated a nostalgia for the old Bedouin days of egalitarianism and political fairness and simplicity, especially among the less privileged members of the tribe. Those themes are well illustrated in `Abdur-Rahman Munif's *Mudun Al-Milh* (*Cities of Salt*).[38]

The major tribes at the founding of the kingdom remain: the `Unayzah, Mutayr, Banu Khalid, Harb, Al-Murrah, Qahtan, and Shammar. There are also some two dozen minor tribes. Several clans form a tribe (seven in the case of Al-Murrah, for example), and several patrilineal lineages form a clan. But the changing social dynamics of the country have in some cases surpassed, overlapped, or conflicted with the traditional structure; tribes are no longer the only politically salient social unit. Traditional merchant families also wield great socioeconomic influence, families like Alireza, Ba Khashab, Bin Ladin, Al-Qusaybi, Jamjun, Jaffali, Kaki, Nasif, `Ulayyan, Ar-Rajhi, and Sulayman. But those families must build alliances with certain princes from the royal family for sponsorship and privileges. And if the social dynamics of the kingdom have undergone important changes, the ideological glue of the kingdom, the Wahhabi doctrine, remains constant.

While Saudi Arabia's influence in regional and international affairs was dramatically expanded by the discovery of its oil, its contributions to Arab cultural and intellectual affairs have been scant. This has never been due to a lack of talent among Saudis but because the political system and its dominant ideology stifle creativity, invention, and critical thinking. As a result, the Saudi government has to buy its influence and prominence.

Saudi Arabia is a new kingdom, but its youth has been a handicap. The royal family often resorts to history in an attempt to steal glory from the Islamic past in order to bestow itself with a measure of respectability that has long eluded it. This explains the two faces of Saudi reputation. The official reputation is one that is largely manufactured and concocted by the royal family for propaganda purposes, and it is maintained by rigidly controlling the media. The other face is the one created and seen by the Arab people and the underground press, which often has far more influence than official discourse. Among the general public, the House of Saud is despised and its members mocked and derided. The history of Saudi Arabia has to take into account the long path of Saudi regime construction and the methods that the royals have used to chart for themselves a respected place at the Arab table.

THREE
Wahhabiyyah

It is not accidental that Saudi Arabia is historically and politically so connected with Islam. It is the birthplace of Islam's Prophet, Muhammad, and is home to the religion's two holiest sites, Mecca and Medina. Because of the immeasurable religious significance of these two sites, since the establishment of the kingdom in 1932, whoever rules the area has to legitimize their power in Islamic terms. That the Saudi state was founded according to the strict doctrine of Wahhabiyyah only added to the link between Saudi Arabia and Islam, because Wahhabiyyah claims to represent the only true, authentic Islam.

As a result of intense (but not always benign) interest in better understanding the Islamic world after 9-11, Wahhabiyyah is no longer an unfamiliar topic in Western culture. Wahhabiyyah is the official state ideology of Saudi Arabia, and the Qur'an serves as the kingdom's constitution. Since Saudi Arabia's inception, the Wahhabiyyah movement has for the most part enjoyed either favorable press or silence from the Arab world. Wahhabiyyah, which has become a controversial political and social phenomenon in Western countries after 9-11, has been blamed for what has been called "Islamic terrorism" or "terrorism in the name of Islam." In the

Arab world, the movement is seen as a quixotic and eccentric deviation from mainstream Islam. Yet there is little discussion of Wahhabiyyah in Arabic because the Saudi government—at least since the death of Nasser and the rise of oil in the early 1970s—has prevented the airing of anti-Wahhabiyyah views. Arab publishing houses either receive direct subsidies or benefit from large contracts with the Saudi government. The Arabic press increasingly has become a beneficiary of Saudi royal wealth. Before the proliferation of satellite stations, Arab governments kept a tight lid on the expression of public views. Only the Shi`ites, who were viciously attacked by the founder of Wahhabiyyah, who considered them infidels, maintained an openly hostile attitude toward Wahhabiyyah. They published anti-Wahhabiyyah literature filled with theological refutation of Saudi religious teachings that was banned by pro-Saudi governments.

Even in English and French, there is scant literature on Wahhabiyyah. One of the early works in any language was published anonymously in French in 1810 (and was only translated into Arabic in 2002): for some reason, Louis Alexandre Olivier de Corancez did not attach his name to his book, *Histoire des Wahabis, Depuis Leur Origine Jusqu'a la Fin de 1809.*[39] Unsurprisingly, the work contains the popular clichéd stereotypes and generalizations about Arabs and Muslims that are common in classical Western Orientalist literature. The first page of the book talks about the Orientals' lack of interest in anything that is not "of immediate benefit to them."[40] Western scholarship showed minimal interest because Wahhabiyyah did not produce a rich body of intellectual work, nor did it capture the imagination of Muslims. It was a state faith, imposed from above by an autocratic government. Only Saudi Arabia and Qatar officially adhere to Wahhabiyyah. Even

Qatar has been moving away from the teachings of the faith.[41] For these reasons, the task of telling the story of Wahhabiyyah fell into the hands of two pro-Saudi propagandists: St. John Philby and the Lebanese writer Amin Rihani. Rihani was the first to write in Arabic about As-Saud's rule.[42] In recent years the late Temple University professor of religion, Isma`il Al-Faruqi, undertook the task of promoting Wahhabiyyah in English, and he translated Muhammad Ibn `Abdul-Wahab's treatise, *Kitab At-Tawhid*.

MUHAMMAD IBN `ABDUL-WAHAB AND HIS DOCTRINE

Wahhabiyyah, or Wahhabism, refers to the doctrine founded by Muhammad Ibn `Abdul-Wahab (1703–92). The followers of the founder are known as Wahhabis, or Wahhabiyyun. It is debatable whether the movement should be considered a reform movement. Some may look at it as a regressive movement in that it fights reforms in the name of fighting "innovations." Members of the movement do not call themselves Wahhabis; they simply, often self-righteously, call themselves Muslims, or *muwahhidun* (literally, unifiers, but it refers to those who insist on the unification of the worship of Allah) or Ahl (Community of) At-Tawhid. But the famous Wahhabi cleric Ibn Baz did not shy away from the term Wahhabis; he considered it an honorary title for those who "are of the people of *tawhid* (unification, and it contains the meaning of strict monotheism), and of the people who are loyal to Allah."[43] The minister of *awqaf* (religious endowment) and Islamic affairs, expressing the defensive Saudi position in the wake of the September 11 attacks stated: "What they call Wahhabiyyah, and they claim that we are on its path, is the path of the predecessors and the crux of religion, and it should not be so named because it is not a new doctrine."[44] However, the movement has been very closely associated with the life and idiosyncratic opinions of its founder, `Abdul-Wahab.

In writing about the founder of Wahhabiyyah, one has to distill the facts from the tale that has been spun by the modern Saudi state in order to present a glamorizing picture of a man who did not leave much of an intellectual imprint. In 2003, Prince Sultan Bin `Abdul-`Aziz, the minister of defense, was talking defensively about Wahhabiyyah and about Muhammad Ibn `Abdul-Wahab. He was reacting to Western press reports critical of the state's faith. He said: "All know who Muhammad Bin `Abdul-Wahab is. He is a man of knowledge and education, and he was Islamically educated in, from what has been said, India, Egypt, Pakistan and finished his studies in his country..."[45] Another Saudi account claims that he also traveled to Iran,[46] although, as Hamid Algar points out, there is no mention of him in the Persian sources of the period in question.[47]

Muhammad Ibn `Abdul-Wahab was born in 1703 in Al-`Uyaynah in Najd. Favorable accounts talk about a precocious kid who memorized the Qur'an before reaching the age of ten and was married by the age of twelve.[48] His father, who apparently was not keen on the religious career of his son, was a local judge belonging to the Hanbalite school of jurisprudence (of the four Sunni schools of jurisprudence, the Hanbalite named after Ahmad Ibn Hanbal, is known as the strictest and most conservative), in a region not renowned for religious scholarship. Muhammad is said to have traveled to Hijaz, Ahsa', and Basrah for study.

In Medina, a center of great learning before it fell under the control of the anti-intellectual clerics of Wahhabiyyah, he was introduced to the works of Ibn Taymiyyah (A.D. 1263–1328),[49] who influenced him a great deal, and who shared with him "a delight in polemics."[50] He is reported to have said: "I know of nobody who approximates Ibn Taymiyyah in the science of hadith (the posthumous collected words and deeds attributed to the Prophet) and interpretation save Ahmad Ibn Hanbal."[51] Ibn Taymiyyah was also a man of the sword: he fought the Crusaders and others in his lifetime, and observed that the foundation of religion is "Qur'an and sword."[52]

It is also significant that Ibn Taymiyyah was unique among "mainstream" Muslim theologians in his praise of the Kharijites. The Khawarij, as they are known in Arabic, were an early Islamic sect that split off from `Ali Ibn Abi Talib (cousin and son-in- law of the Prophet, and the founder of the Shi`ite group; the name Shi`ite is Arabic for "the partisans of" `Ali) during his disputes with the Companions of the Prophet.[53] The Khawarij were perhaps the first group of Muslims to sanction, on theological grounds, the murder of fellow Muslims. Some Kharijite splinter sects even permitted the killing of the children of "deviant" Muslims. In Islamic history, the Khawarij are often categorized as fanatical, and some of their practices may have been emulated by armed groups like Al-Qa`idah.[54] On the Khawarij, Ibn Taymiyyah said: "Although they have deviated in religion, they do not lie but are known as truthful and they only cite the sound hadiths. But they were ignorant and misguided in their innovation, but their innovation was not due to *zandaqah* [the ideas of a group of freethinking antimonotheists in Islamic history who were influenced by *"concepts philosophiques helleniques et rationnels"*][55] or atheism, but to misguidedness and ignorance."[56]

Today, Ibn Taymiyyah's thought and practice can be seen

as a key philosophical predecessor of contemporary Islamic fundamentalism, and one can trace some of Wahhabiyyah's core ideas back to his prolific writings. His most important contribution to present-day militant ideologies, like those of Al-Qa`idah, is his belief that misguided Muslims—those who do not abide by (his interpretation of) Shari`ah (the body of Islamic laws)—should be fought as if they were infidels. Followers asked him about the appropriateness of fighting the Tatars, who were Muslims, and he issued a fatwa (a binding religious edict) to the effect that "they should be fought until they abide by the laws."[57] But in fairness to Taymiyyah, and despite his extreme conservatism and textualism in treating the Qur'an, he was far more original in dealing with matters of personal status laws and matters of "the branches" of Islamic laws. He, for example, was alone in believing that the fire of hell is not eternal, but that its victims will eventually be sent to heaven.[58] He made many enemies, and he was persecuted and died in jail.

Ibn Taymiyyah was, like Wahhabiyyah later, concerned with the ramifications of prayer in terms of the strict monotheism that sums up the message of Islam.[59] It is easy to discern the influence of Taymiyyah on `Abdul-Wahab, and it can be stated that the latter was a fanatical and extremist devotee of the former. Some of the issues that would later occupy the mind and life of `Abdul-Wahab were tackled, with less intensity perhaps, by Ibn Taymiyyah. Taymiyyah was uncompromising in his attacks on Sufis (Islamic mystics), and he compared some of them to infidels and pagans,[60] although as Algar points out, he—unlike Muhammad `Abdul-Wahab—"did not reject [Sufism] *in toto*."[61] Similarly, there was another doctrine that Wahhabiyyah would later stretch to extremes: Taymiyyah permitted Muslims to seek the intercession of the

Prophet in their prayer, but only when the Prophet was alive, and he forbade the practice—very common among Muslims—after Muhammad's death. He similarly forbade Muslims from making requests in their visits to the tombs of holy people, including the tomb of the Prophet.[62] Furthermore, Wahhabiyyah's doctrine of anti-Shi`ism can also be traced to Ibn Taymiyyah's attribution of the first *fit-nah* (literally, "sedition," but it means here civil strife) in Islam to Shi`ism.[63] He was also an influence on the puritanism and prudishness that characterized the thought and practice of modern Wahhabiyyah. He led an ascetic lifestyle, which is alien to the life of the Prophet and the teachings of Islam. Islam, unlike the ascetic ideal of Christianity that Nietzsche so detested, called on the believers to enjoy the pleasures of the earth. Ibn Taymiyyah did not marry and abstained from even enjoying the beauty of nature. In this regard he was closer to Saint Augustine than to mainstream Islamic jurists.

Having learned some Sunni Islamic theology, `Abdul-Wahab aimed toward Basrah, hoping to teach Shi`ites some lessons. On his experience in Basrah, which was, and still is, predominantly Shi`ite, he is said to have observed, in anticipation of his future doctrine: "There were people from the pagans of Basrah who used to bring me problematiques, and I would say in their presence that only Allah's worship is appropriate, and they would get astonished, and not say a word."[64] However, his audience may not have been impressed with his talents. He was forcibly expelled from Basrah by angry Shi`ites, according to the accounts of his adherents.[65] In fact, his twentieth-century official interpreter states that some clerics of Basrah revolted and attacked him.[66] Not only did he alienate the Shi`ite clerics, but contemporary accounts do not speak of congruence between Muhammad's early views and those of his father or his brother,

Sulayman (the author of a well-known pioneering refutation of Wahhabiyyah).[67] His father had some fight with his son,[68] and along with his other son, Sulayman, saw signs of "doctrinal deviance in him at a quite early age."[69] The father was punished for the views of the son, and the family moved to Huraymilah. After his father's death in 1740 and after a failed assassination attempt that not even his sympathetic biographer denies, Muhammad moved back to Al-`Uyaynah.[70] He had to persuade members of his community, and he realized, as he himself commented, "words are not sufficient."[71] His father's death must have removed a restraint, as he then began a zealous campaign against the enemies of Islam as he identified them. He ordered that all tombstones and mosques built over the tombs of the dead be destroyed, and that trees used as sites for votive offerings be cut. Even the tombs of holy men, including the dome of a companion of the Prophet, Zayd Bin Al-Khattab, were not spared.

Muhammad, however, attained his fame, so to say, by way of the public execution of a woman who allegedly confessed her adultery. `Abdul-Wahab arranged for four male witnesses, and the woman's fate was sealed with Muhammad's verdict. He ordered that she be tied down and stoned to death. The news spread, and the people of Ahsa' nearly revolted, according to Rihani. The prince of the region wrote to the local ruler that Muhammad had to be stopped, or be killed.[72] Muhammad, of course, was insistent on continuing to propagate his message, which he referred to as *tawhid* (Arabic for unification, or unity, and it carries a multitude of meanings in Islamic theology). As threats to his life increased, Muhammad, at the age of forty-two, took the decision to move. He relocated on foot to Dir`iyyah, a small market town that was under the rule of Muhammad Bin Sa`ud. Apparently, the Saudi ruler initially expressed reservations about meeting the famed preacher. Bin Sa`ud's wife changed his mind about `Abdul-Wahab by telling him: "This man was led toward us by Allah, and he is a great find, so take advantage of what Allah has made exclusively yours."[73] Thereupon, Prince Muhammad Bin Sa`ud walked to Muhammad Ibn `Abdul-Wahab and in 1744 struck a firm alliance that remains at the core of the Saudi state to this very day: the alliance between the House of Sa`ud and the House of Ash-Shaykh (as the contemporary descendants of `Abdul-Wahab are known). `Abdul-Wahab settled and began a campaign of jihad. Jihad means holy struggle in general, but here it refers to the holy war that the two men led in Arabia. Their war continued into the last century until the Saudi kingdom was founded.

`Abdul-Wahab, unlike Islamic thinkers and jurists of his time, did not leave a body of work. His only book, which is really a booklet, is *Kitab at-Tawhid* (The Book of Tawhid). It is a mere collection of hadiths, which are the sayings or deeds attributed to the Prophet. Muslims consider the hadiths to be second only to the Qur'an in authority and as a source of Islamic jurisprudence. One cannot compare the scant writings of `Abdul-Wahab to the vast intellectual and polemical body of works of his real mentor, Ibn Taymiyyah.[74] The ideas of `Abdul-Wahab can be summarized by references to *tawhid*, which had at least three meanings for him: the first refers to the exclusive quality of lordship of the world to Allah; the second refers to the exclusive association of the divine names and attributes with Allah only ("even for example, *karim* [generous]"),[75] and the third refers to the concentration of worship in God alone.[76] In `Abdul-Wahab's words, "worship is *tawhid*."[77] But `Abdul-Wahab applied everything dogmatically, and any disagreements that he had with any other

Muslims he easily and casually attributed to Satan. He believed that even average Muslims' love for the "benevolent predecessors"[78] was the product of a devious satanic plot,[79] and that any interpretations and opinions that were not in his version of Sunnah (path of the Prophet) were part of Satan's plan.[80] This explains the zeal with which `Abdul-Wahab, with the aid of the Sauds, went about waging wars, in the name of jihad, against fellow Muslims in Arabia and beyond. For him, war against Muslims who were in error was not only permissible, it was "obligatory."[81] Muslims who did not accept his doctrine were no longer to be considered Muslims but rather *mushrikun* (polytheists). He added that the Qur'an is clear that polytheism is the only unforgivable sin in Islam, and that God forgives all sins short of polytheism: "Allah does not forgive the association of other gods in his worship, and he forgives short of that anybody, and he who associates other gods with Allah has strayed far, far away."[82]

None other than Muhammad `Abdul-Wahab's own brother, Sulayman, quickly detected the dangerous repercussions of the beliefs of this new doctrine. Sulayman wrote the first anti-Wahhabiyyah tract, which remains banned in Saudi Arabia. Shi`ites, in their polemics against Wahhabiyyah, found the text useful, and the identity of the author has been very damaging to the founder of the doctrine. So incensed was `Abdul-Wahab about his brother's criticisms that when he found a Muslim promoting Sulayman's book, he had him executed on the spot.[83] Sulayman's book suggests that he was aghast at the consequences of his brother's beliefs. He begins his work by questioning his brother's credentials as an interpreter of Islamic texts. He lists a number of essential ingredients that all scholars of religion should have, clearly implying that his brother did not have the knowledge or the wisdom to engage in his religious change agenda.[84] He then expresses his outrage that, according to Muhammad's doctrine, a Muslim who attests that there is no God but God (the first pillar of the Islamic faith); who performs prayer, commits almsgiving, fasts during Ramadan, and performs the hajj (pilgrimage to Mecca); who believes in God, the holy books, messengers, and angels; and who is committed to all the rituals of Islam can still be considered a *kafir* (infidel) by Wahhabi standards if he does not share the opinions of `Abdul-Wahab.[85] Sulayman's tone shifts from academic to outright angry, and he asks his brother: "Verify to us where have you obtained your doctrine? This!"[86] He also reminds the adherents of Wahhabiyyah that if they were trying to follow the words of Ibn Taymiyyah and Ibn Qayyim Al-Jawziyyah (1292–1350, devout student of Taymiyyah), they should have known that the two would not approve of the casual *takfir* (declaration of a fellow Muslim's infidelity).[87] Sulayman did not exaggerate when he said that whoever disagrees with his brother is declared a *kafir*.

Muhammad `Abdul-Wahab's views and opinions did not originally excite or persuade the body of Muslim scholars, not even those of Najd who were followers of Ibn Taymiyyah. He struck many of them as a strident and uncompromising zealot, as when he declared that whoever asks for the intercession of the Prophet is committing a sin equal to that of asking for the intercession of worshipped idols.[88] His generalizations offended many Muslims. Such generalizations, like the following, are still offensive to many today: "Most people have been toyed with by Satan, and he beautified polytheism [for them]."[89] Throughout his lifetime he never wavered from calling all other Muslims *mushrikun*. In fact, some of his contemporaries in Najd declared him guilty of *riddah* (apostasy) and strongly objected to his favorite method of *takfir*.[90] A certain `alim` (doctor of religion, plural `ulama'`) from Riyadh wrote a letter to the people of Basrah and Ahsa' against `Abdul-Wahab. In this letter he reminded them that "he who does not agree with him on everything…is decisively declared an infidel; and he who agrees with him and believes him in everything he says, he says: 'you are *muwahhid*' [one who believes in unity of God's worship]."[91] Another wrote that `Abdul-Wahab "has declared the infidelity of the entire *ummah* [community of Muslims]; no, by Allah, he has falsified the prophets and ruled that they and their nations are polytheists."[92]

There are contradictions between Wahhabiyyah and mainstream Islam, including conflicts with most conservative branches of Sunni jurisprudence, such as the Hanbalite school. One of these contradictions is that Islam has always allowed for a measure of flexibility and pragmatism, and that Islamic laws allow for what is called *hiyal* (tricks), which are methods to violate certain Islamic rules without seeming to really violate them. This, for example, allowed Muslims to engage in arts (although early Muslim jurists banned it), to engage in capitalistic transactions (although Islam banned usury), or even to deviate from the righteous path if the person's excuse was mere ignorance.[93] Wahhabiyyah, in contrast, is inflexible; it rejects ignorance as a reason for forgiveness or leniency.[94]

The alliance between the Sauds and `Abdul-Wahab has produced a politically quiescent and conservative school of political thought that urges obedience to the rulers, within a Wahhabi doctrine. `Abdul-Wahab forbade revolt against the rulers, regardless of the policies and conduct of those rulers. This was contrary to the beliefs of his intellectual mentor, who had permitted dissent and rebellion against rulers, under certain conditions.[95] This has been the most useful element of

Wahhabism for the House of Saud. `Abdul-Wahab urged absolute obedience to the rulers in all of their policies and commands, provided that they ("they" have to be men, of course, for `Abdul-Wahab, and for Sunni and Shi`ite jurisprudence) do not order a violation of Allah's will.[96] This doctrine has guaranteed the subservience of the Wahhabi religious authorities to the royal family of the kingdom, especially when the clerical establishment has been led by descendants of `Abdul-Wahab (those descendants known as the House of Shaykh). Along those lines, the head of Hay'at Kibar Al-`Ulama' (literally, the Body of Senior `Ulama'), which is the highest religious authority in the kingdom, `Abdul-`Aziz Bin `Abdullah Al Ash-Shaykh (a descendant of Muhammad Ibn `Abdul-Wahab) declared in August 2003—probably in response to intense criticisms within the kingdom of the royal family—that "rulers, even if unjust, should be obeyed."[97] Thus, the formula for the alliance between the two sides, which was cemented at the time of `Abdul-Wahab, has survived to this very day.

There is also the Islamic issue of *bid`ah* (literally, innovation, *bida`* in plural). In Wahhabi terminology this word is of tremendous importance; Hamid Algar calls its usage "capricious and undiscriminating."[98] Originally, the word in Arabic referred only to the act of initiation, of starting something new.[99] In the worldview of Wahhabiyyah, *bida`* refers to all that has happened in Islamic history after the passing of the first three centuries. Every change since that time is condemned. Thus, for example, reading the Qur'an aloud, for a purpose other than the public call for prayers from a mosque, is a *bid`ah*.[100] As Algar points out, some scholars, like Shafi`i `Izz Ad-Din Bin `Abdus-Salam, spoke of "a good innovation," but `Abdul-Wahab spoke only of negative innovations.[101] However, even if one is to follow the path of some school of jurisprudence founded during the glorified first three centuries of Islam, one is committing the condemned act of *bid`ah*, because none of those schools agree in every instance with 'Abdul-Wahab.

`Abdul-Wahab did not confine himself to a revolution in words. He also led, in alliance with Ibn Sa`ud, a violent campaign of forced conversion. In 1746 (Algar puts the date at A.H. 1159, but Rihani puts it at A.H. 1157), the Saudi-Wahhabi alliance declared jihad against "the polytheists" (i.e., other Muslims in Arabia and beyond): for them, it was a war of Muslims against pagans. Not all were quick to succumb to the violent cause. When Ibn Sa`ud called on his friend Ibn Dawwas to join the "religion of unification," the friend blurted out: "Who is this son of Muqrin to carry the keys to heaven and to warn people with the fire [of hell]?"[102] Najd was the first target for conquest. `Abdul-Wahab did not live to see the conquest of Mecca; he died twelve years earlier, in 1791 (1792 in Rihani).[103] The conquest of Hijaz was the most important, but the Saudi-Wahhabi alliance set its sight on the Shi`ites to the north in Iraq. `Abdul-Wahab would refer to Shi`ites as *rawafid* (rejectionists), which remains part of the current terminology in both Wahhabi and Al-Qa`idah literature. What transpired in the campaign against the Shi`ites of southern Iraq, especially in the holy city of Karbala', which contains the burial site of Imam Husayn (grandson of the Prophet, and the great martyr of Shi`ism), was nothing short of a massacre. A Wahhabi historian tells the story:

> In the year 1216, Sa`ud [son of `Abdul-`Aziz] set out with his divinely supported army and cavalry that he had recruited from both the city dwellers and nomads of Najd, from the south, from the Hijaz, Tihama and elsewhere. He made for Karbala and

began hostilities against the people of the city of Al-Husayn.... The Muslims [i.e., the Wahhabis] scaled the walls, entered the city by force, and killed the majority of its people in the markets and in their homes. Then they destroyed the dome placed over the grave of Al-Husayn by those who believe in such things. They took over whatever they found inside the dome and its surroundings. They took the grille surrounding the tomb, which was encrusted with emeralds, rubies, and other jewels. They took everything they found in the town: different types of property, weapons, clothing, carpets, gold, silver, precious copies of the Qur'an, as well as much else—more than can be enumerated. They stayed in Karbala for no more than a morning, leaving around midday with all the property they had gathered and having killed about two thousand people. Then Sa`ud departed by way of Al-Ma' Al-Abyad. He had the booty assembled in front of him. He deducted one fifth for himself and then distributed the rest among the Muslims [i.e., the Wahhabis], giving a single share to each foot soldier and a double share to each horseman. Then he returned home.[104]

Thus we learn of "holy war," Wahhabi style. Other campaigns of plunder, pillage, and mayhem followed. The attack on Mecca and Medina also included the destruction of the gravestones and tombs of close companions and wives of the Prophet. The Ottomans became concerned; the holy sites of Mecca and Medina constituted important sources of legitimacy of the sultan. Sa`ud, upon entering Mecca, tried to preempt any Ottoman action; he dispatched a message to Sultan

Salim informing him "he has destroyed the likes of pagan idols."[105] The leading clerics of Mecca were forced to issue a statement in which they stated that "this religion [sic] that was founded by Ash-Shaykh Muhammad Bin `Abdul-Wahab, may God have mercy upon him, and to which he invited the Imam of the Muslims Sa`ud Bin `Abdul-`Aziz, and which contained the unification of the worship of God and the rejection of polytheism...is the indubitable righteousness."[106] But Wahhabi-Saudi success did not last long. By 1812 an Egyptian army, sent to liberate the holy places by order of the Ottoman sultan, landed in Yanbu`, and by 1819 the Sauds were defeated—they were pushed out of Hijaz, and their capital (Dir`iyyah) was sacked. Even sympathetic chroniclers concede that this new Saudi state relied too much on force alone: in the words of King `Abdul-`Aziz's advisor Hafidh Wahbah, the "state was reliant more on military force than on hearts."[107] Saud also grew defiant and provocative toward the Egyptians and Ottomans. Some Najdite `ulama' (clerics) blamed the House of Shaykh (the family of `Abdul-Wahab) for the destruction and devastation that befell the region as a result of alienating the population with their system of justice and bloody vengeance.[108] Saud, whose son was put to death by the Ottomans, developed a reputation for brutality. The sympathetic Wahbah heard this account from King `Abdul-`Aziz: "He once imprisoned some of the elders of Mutyar, so other elders came to ask for his mercy. He detected some defiance in them, so he ordered that they be beheaded. He then brought their heads to his dinner table, and ordered their cousins (who also came to ask for his mercy) to eat from that table."[109] We also learn from this account the important information that he was elegant and always liked to be perfumed.[110]

The House of Saud did not settle for defeat. They made various efforts in the nineteenth century to reclaim their past glory, but internal disputes and interfamily feuds prevented the family from establishing its control over the whole of Arabia or the holy places. That task was undertaken by the founder of the modern kingdom, King `Abdul-`Aziz.

WAHHABISM IN THE TWENTIETH CENTURY: THE CASE OF IBN BAZ

Since forging it, the Saudi royal family has stuck to the bargain that was first struck between Ibn Saud and `Abdul-Wahab. It is said that when the two finalized their agreement, Ibn Saud assured `Abdul-Wahab that he would stick by him even "if the whole of Najd came tumbling down over us."[111] In fact, the royal family has loyally followed the practice of appointing a member of the House of Shaykh (the family of the descendants of Muhammad Ibn `Abdul-Wahab) as the grand mufti of the kingdom (the highest Sunni religious authority in a country and the one who is the most authoritative in issuing fatwas).[112] Only one person has been the exception: `Abdul-`Aziz Bin `Abdullah Bin Baz, better known as Ibn Baz (1912–99). This most senior of contemporary Saudi Wahhabi `ulama' was born in Riyadh; he did not receive formal education but studied under various clerics, many of whom were direct descendants of Muhammad `Abdul-Wahab himself. He lost his eyesight early in life but persevered in his studies and quickly assumed positions of Islamic judgeships, while teaching at Islamic Shari`ah (Islamic laws) colleges in the kingdom. In A.H. 1318 (1961), he was appointed vice president of the Islamic University in Medina and became its head in 1970. He was appointed chairperson of the Administrations of

[Religious] Scientific Research and Ifta' (the issuance of religious edicts), Da`wah (propagation), and Irshad (guidance), at the rank of minister. In 1993, he was appointed grand mufti. He became the first person to ever hold that position who was not a member of the House of Shaykh, and King Fahd promptly appointed Shaykh `Abdul-`Aziz Al Ash-Shaykh as his successor.

Ibn Baz has played a very important role in religious and political legitimization for the House of Saud. His obscurantist views, in tune with early Wahhabi teachings and the suspicion that the new is a manifestation of hidden Satanic influences, made him credible among the faithful Wahhabi crowd. Even the militant extremes of Islamic fundamentalists, like those drawn to Al-Qa`idah, continued to look up to him as a source of religious inspiration and wisdom until the first Gulf War, when he covered for the royal family when they invited U.S. troops to the kingdom. Bin Ladin wrote him a personal letter in which he expressed respect but urged him to break with the royal family, listing a litany of complaints, some of which included edicts by Ibn Baz that facilitated the rule of the House of Saud. The letter was written in 1994, and in it Bin Ladin does not seem to break completely with Ibn Baz. Though it is rarely mentioned, Bin Ladin does not practice a splinter form of Wahhabi Islam; he practices the official Saudi ideology—Wahhabi—and has attempted to hold the Saudi royals accountable to it. Bin Ladin only broke with the Saudi establishment over foreign policy. In fact, in urging Ibn Baz to break with the king, Bin Ladin cites a previous fatwa that had been issued by Ibn Baz against peace with Israel.[113] In the letter, however, he also listed a number of domestic violations by the royal family (corruption, inclination toward peace with "the Jews," the utilization of usury in Saudi banking, etc.). Such was the stand-

ing of Ibn Baz among the militants of the Salafiyyah (those
Muslim fundamentalists who follow the early example of "the
benevolent" *salaf* [predecessors, literally]) type, despite all evidence that such a break was unlikely.

Bin Ladin did not shy away from reminding the shaykh of
his responsibilities as an independent scholar of religion—
independent in theory, that is. Bin Ladin wrote: "We want
from the aforementioned to remind you of your responsibilities toward religion and toward the nation, and we wish to
alert you to your great responsibilities."[114] Bin Ladin presents
for the eyes of the shaykh a laundry list of Saudi "crimes and
misdeeds from the wearing of the cross by King Fahd" (it was
not clear what he meant by that, but this apparently is a
widely circulated story among Saudi dissidents) and the prevailing corruption of the family to the alliance with "Christian
and Jewish" forces and the allowance of banking transactions
within the kingdom.

During the most serious political crises of legitimacy the
royal family faced, whether in 1979 during the Mecca rebellion or in 1990 when the kingdom "invited" U.S. troops, Ibn
Baz came to the rescue. His absence from the scene (i.e., his
death) coincided with the most severe religious crisis (i.e., the
aftermath of September 11) that the kingdom has had to face,
and has been facing since at least 1991, with the controversial
decision to deploy U.S. troops on Saudi lands. Ibn Baz, with his
standing within the clerical establishment and within the
ranks of the fundamentalist dissidents, could have accorded
more religio-political legitimacy to the kingdom during those
recent crucial years of trouble and instability.

However, Ibn Baz is responsible for the reactionary religion—or version of religion—that has been consolidated in
Saudi Arabia. He is responsible for the promotion and propa-

gation of an extremely exclusivist and conservative interpretation of Islam through the standpoint of Wahhabiyyah. His writings constitute an elaboration on the thought of `Abdul-Wahab, with a defiant resistance to accommodate the changes of the modern world. He is still remembered for issuing a fatwa in which he disputed the story of the landing on the moon, although, in fairness to him, he argued that it should be possible for people to land on the moon someday because the "*jinns* [floating spirits or demons] were able to ascend to the skies until they touched it."[115] His rulings included the declaration of infidelity (*takfir*) of Muslims who do not believe those stories about the Prophet that defy logic; the ban on pictures,[116] statues, and archaeological relics; the ban on prayer behind a man dressed in a suit and tie; the rejection of the rotation of the earth; the ban on perfume; and the ban on singing and music.[117] The perpetuation of the strict and puritanical moral order in Saudi Arabia throughout the last century, and beyond, has been facilitated and rationalized by Ibn Baz.

His legacy is still particularly felt in the laws and regulations pertaining to women in Saudi Arabia. He had resisted all efforts of reform and was adamant not to compromise Wahhabiyyah's sexist and misogynist standards; in fact, he may be responsible for firmly reinforcing the ban against women driving in the kingdom. Regarding this issue, he had said, "It is known that it leads to misdeeds known by its advocates, like the prohibited seclusion with a woman, and the incautious mixing with men, and including the perpetration of taboos for which these things are banned...."[118] He was consistent on imposing conditions and restraints on women's ability to move freely in space: he was opposed to the wife leaving the house without the husband's permission. He, along with the other members of the authoritative Permanent Committee for [Religious] Scientific Research and Ifta', stated clearly: "If a woman wants to leave the house of her husband, she is to tell him of her destination, and he would authorize her to leave provided that no harm is done in this regard, and he is better aware of her interests."[119] He also urged a husband, who is entitled to hit his wife (in cases of her disobedience), to do so but without hitting her "harshly" (*ghayra mubarrahin*).[120] But Ibn Baz was lenient enough to permit women to wear watches during periods of mourning, although he personally preferred that they avoid wearing them.[121] Muslim women, he stated, have to be seen by fellow female Muslim physicians. If one is not available, a Muslim male physician may examine her but in the presence of her husband or a male guardian, "for fear of *fitnah* [sedition] or that which cannot be praised."[122] Ibn Baz also prohibited women from wearing high heels (he did not issue an edict on its permissibility for men). He, in the authority of the aforementioned Permanent Committee, stated: "The wearing of high heels is impermissible because it may lead the woman to fall, and a human being is ordered by Islamic laws to avoid risks…and it shows the stature of the woman and her behind more prominently, and there is in this deception and display of some ornaments that believing women were prohibited from…."[123]

But Ibn Baz's strictness also applied to men. He was generally quite displeased with men wearing Western clothes. He also believed in strict and separate dress codes for men and women, the exchange of clothes being highly prohibited. On men's clothing, he stated, regarding the suit and tie: "If that clothing does not identify the pudendum because it is loose, and if it does not reveal what is behind it due to thickness, then a man can pray while wearing it, but if it reveals what is behind, as in seeing the pudendum, then one cannot pray in it, and if the pudendum is identified, then prayer in it should be avoided."[124] He also forbade smoking because it is *haram* (religiously impermissible) and is one of the *khaba'ith* (an old Qur'anic word that means condemned deeds).[125] Members of the royal family who smoke have to do so in private; Crown Prince `Abdullah, for example, smokes regularly but only in private.[126]

Ibn Baz's strictness extended to all facets of life; he banned those who study martial arts from bowing to each other because bowing is "a salutation of worship, and worship is only for God alone."[127] He is equally strict on the belief systems of Muslim youths; this has made him a very useful tool in the Saudi-American alliance against communism during the Cold War. His ruling in this regard is quite unambiguous: "Those who call for socialism or communism or other destructive doctrines that are contrary to the rule of Islam, are *akfar* (more unbelieving, or more of infidels) than Jews and Christians, because they are atheists who do not believe in God or in the hereafter. It is not permissible for any of them to be made a preacher or imam in any of the Muslim mosques and it is not appropriate for people to pray behind them."[128] Ibn Baz's moral wrath also applied to those who live under secular laws, "those who step outside the circle of Islam and consequently become unjust and lascivious infidels."[129]

Ibn Baz's credibility suffered a great deal among fundamentalist and Wahhabi ranks when he sanctioned the invitation of U.S. troops to the kingdom in 1990. He had a history of fanatical hostility to Jews and Christians—all Jews and Christians. Before the deployment of U.S. troops during "Operation Desert Shield," if not earlier, Ibn Baz had urged in sermons and fatwas the hatred of all Jews and Christians. He once wrote:

Some local newspapers have published opinions of some people to the effect that "We do not harbor hostility to Jews and Judaism and that we respect all monotheistic religions...." And as this talk regarding Jews and Judaism clashes blatantly with the dear Book and the pure Sunnah, and conflicts with the Islamic doctrine, and one fears that this may deceive some people, it is important to alert to what it contained of error.... I say: The Book and Sunnah and the consensus of Muslims indicate that it is incumbent upon Muslims to take as enemies the infidel Jews and Christians and other polytheists, and to avoid their amiability or take them as guardians as He, glory be to Him, maintained in His book.[130]

However, Ibn Baz may not have been as principled in his hostility to Jews and Christians as his earlier edicts may have led us to believe: when prompted by the royal family—which was facing a crisis of political legitimacy the likes of which had not been seen since the 1979 Mecca rebellion—Ibn Baz delivered. He issued a fatwa permitting the government to seek aid from the United States and other countries. He said, in justification, that what "occurred from the standpoint of the Saudi government due to the events produced by the injustice at the hand of the president of Iraq vis-à-vis Kuwait, regarding its resort to a group of armies from different peoples of Muslims *and others* [my italics] to deter aggression and to defend the homeland, is permissible and even conditioned by necessity, and necessity leads the kingdom to undertake this obligation because defending peace and Muslims and the sanctity of homeland and its people is necessary."[131] The

Committee of Senior Clerics did the same, and praised the king for inviting "qualified forces."[132]

In all such statements, even by members of the royal family, the identity of the troops, most of which were Americans, were kept confidential. Despite this attempt at discretion, the public knew. Official media referred to them as "Arab, Muslim, and other friendly forces" assisting the kingdom. The veil of secrecy shrouding the Saudi alliance with the United States was lifted only after 9-11, but that did not help the kingdom. At the same time that pressures mounted to expel U.S. forces from the kingdom, the American secretary of defense announced that U.S. troops stationed in the kingdom would be redeployed to neighboring countries immediately after the collapse of Saddam's regime. He added that American "advisors" would remain in the kingdom.

The attention that 9-11 has brought to Wahhabiyyah has been embarrassing to the royal family, not only because it puts Saudi foreign diplomats on the defensive about Wahhabiyyah and its repressiveness but also because the Arabic press, especially the live shows on Arab satellite stations, have carried voices that have mocked and criticized Wahhabiyyah by name.[133] For Bin Ladin's Arab critics, the language that he speaks is not different from that of Ibn Baz and the religious establishment in the kingdom. Shi`ites have been most prolific in their attacks on Wahhabiyyah. This makes intuitive sense, given the condescension and disdain with which Shi`ites are treated in the Saudi state and in Wahhabiyyah religious literature. Ibn Baz and his contemporaries continued the tradition of anti-Shi`ite propaganda: Ibn Baz forbade prayers behind Zaydiyyah (Shi`ite sect of Yemen) adherents,[134] and his colleague Ibn `Uthaymin stated regarding Shi`ites:

It is more correct to say rafidah (rejectionists) because
their partisanship (tashayyu`uhum) for `Ali Ibn Abi
Talib, may God be satisfied with him, is an extreme
and ultra partisanship...and rejectionists, as they
were described by Shaykh of Islam Ibn Taymiyyah...
are the most lying of various sects of passion, and the
most polytheist, and none of the people of passion
are more lying than them, and more remote from
monotheism...and their danger on Islam is very great
indeed, and they were the reason behind the fall of
the caliphate in Baghdad.[135]

The power of Ibn Baz is now confined to his legacy; the
descendants of `Abdul-Wahab are back in the saddle of reli-
gious leadership in the kingdom. None of them has the standing of Ibn Baz, and they have so far proven subservient to the
king and the crown prince during the turbulent post–9-11
alliance with Washington. It is not clear that the royal family
can respond to the demands for liberalization and openness
coming not only from international pressure but also from liberal voices within the kingdom. When one such liberal voice,
Jamal Al-Khashuqji, former editor-in-chief of *Al-Watan*, went
too far in his mockery of Saudi clerics in 2003, the clerical
establishment intervened: seven senior clerics submitted a
petition to the crown prince complaining about *Al-Watan*'s
coverage of the Riyadh bombings and urged the government to
oust Al-Khashuqji.[136] He was unceremoniously dismissed from
his position, without any explanation from the government,
which is typical of how things go in Saudi Arabia. (He later
became a media advisor to the Saudi ambassador in London.)

And when they are needed, the descendants of `Abdul-
Wahab can still come to the rescue of the House of Saud. In

March 2004, days after the arrest of liberal reformers, the Saudi mufti, `Abdul-`Aziz Al Ash-Shaykh, stated that second to the national religion coming under threat, the worst thing that could happen to a nation would be for harm to come to its "leadership and officials, [which would lead to] the loss of the nation and the disturbance of criteria, and then chaos would prevail." He again then urged people to obey their leaders.[137] This act of fealty on the part of the House of Shaykh comes at a time when liberal reformers and fundamentalist clerics are maneuvering for power and influence in the emerging yet indefinite formula of power rearrangement within the kingdom.

As a result of the U.S. destabilization of Iraq, the rising Shi`ite power there will pose a threat to Wahhabi influence: the Shi`ite religious schools of Najaf and Karbala are destined to restore some of their past role in production and education, and this will include attacks on the Wahhabiyyah position. How can Saudi Arabia continue to meet the intense demands of its state religious institutions and the intense demands of the United States? And how can it continue to spread its influence around the world by virtue of its wealth, without seeming to encourage an ideology that is directly at odds with the U.S. war against terrorism? The slogans and themes of U.S. propaganda during the Cold War have changed; now the very militant Islamic ideology that once proved so useful for the U.S. campaign against the Soviet Union is focused directly against the United States. But to understand the difficult and awkward position that the House of Saud finds itself in, one has to closely examine the evolution of the Saudi state and the succession of Saudi kings and their subsequent challenges.

FOUR

Founding and Evolution of State

THE FOUNDER

The creation of the Saudi state in the twentieth century owes much to the power and personality of King `Abdul-`Aziz. As much as Saudi propaganda wishes to underline the heroic significance of the state's founder, there is much in contemporary Saudi history, and in the tale of the founding of the kingdom, about the role of superpower rivalry and interregional intrigues. After all, foreign powers were present, and by 1900 "most of the coastal rulers of the peninsula from Kuwait to Muscat had already signed protection treaties with Britain."[138] The Arabian interior had to wait for World War I, when Britain extended its influence farther. This is the stuff of which Middle East history is made; the classical game of the Eastern question included the entanglement of outside powers with indigenous forces and their impact on local and international developments.[139] One pro-Saudi author credits the entire enterprise of Saudi victory (against their enemies) and the subsequent creation of the modern state to "the extraordinary military prowess and statesmanship of just one remarkable man, His Majesty King Abdul Aziz Ibn Saud."[140]

The legend of Ibn Saud (as King `Abdul-`Aziz has been known in the West) is the product of a very careful and elaborate tale of propaganda woven primarily through the efforts of St. John Philby and Lebanese writer Amin Rihani. Rihani introduced Arabia and its remote regions to Arab readers, and his book *Muluk Al-ʿArab* (*The Kings of the Arabs*) is a tribute to every royalty and princely authority that he met in his travels in the regions. Of ʿAbdul-ʿAziz, he tells us: "I have hereby met all the princes of the Arabs and have not found among them somebody bigger than this man. I do not take a risk nor do I exaggerate in what I say. He indeed is great: great in his handshake, smile, talk, looks, and even in the way he hits the ground with his cane...."[141]

What we know for sure is this: ʿAbdul-ʿAziz lived in exile with his father under the protection of the House of Sabah in Kuwait after the family fled Riyadh in 1890. With a force of forty (some sources say sixty) men, Ibn returned to his home and captured Riyadh in 1902. From this base, Ibn Saud expanded his influence and launched wars against other regions in Najd. But it cannot be said that Ibn Saud's victories were won entirely on his own; his relationship with the royal family in Kuwait provided indirect British support, especially when the House of Rashid tried to reclaim Riyadh in A.H. 1320.[142] And when Ibn Saud moved east toward Hasa, Britain either did not interfere[143] or gave support,[144] depending on the source one reads. In any case, Britain did not make its objections, if it had any, known at the time, though Saudi-British contacts go all the way back to 1865.

Philby notes that Ibn Saud became convinced of the value of a British alliance as early as 1904.[145] His enemies' (the Ar-Rashids') alliance with the Ottomans brought the British closer to him. The control of Al-Hasa placed a Shiʿite community under the Wahhabi and anti-Shiʿite rule of Ibn Saud. According to at least one source, Ibn Saud promised religious freedom for the community, a promise that has been broken flagrantly, regularly, and consistently by Ibn Saud and every one of his successors.[146] His position strengthened in 1915 when Ibn Saud signed the Anglo-Saudi Treaty, in which the British acknowledged Saudi control over Najd, Hasa, Qatif, and Jubayl.[147]

Even the success of Ibn Saud against the Hashemites can be understood in terms of a British policy; the Hashemites, after all, were too ambitious—or too grandiose in their ambitions—for British tastes. The dream of a grand Arab empire under Sharif Husayn (the head of the Hashemites) did not go well with British colonial plans for the Middle East after World War I, their promises to the Arabs notwithstanding. In this context, Ibn Saud directed himself toward the Hijaz, given the great religious significance of the holy places and the added religio-political legitimacy. As Wahhabis considered adoption of Wahhabiyyah—even by Muslims—a conversion from polytheism to Islam, it is certain that Ibn Saud's campaign in Hijaz (and elsewhere in Arabia) was one based on forced "conversion" through butchery and brutality. There are no reliable figures for the number of people slaughtered as a result of the Wahhabi campaign that led to the founding of Saudi Arabia, but the figure of four hundred thousand killed and wounded (cited by Algar[148] and based on Abursih[149]) seems to be an exaggeration. It is safe to assume that thousands of people were mercilessly killed in the Saudi campaigns, and scores of women and men were enslaved.[150] Ibn Saud himself admitted the role of violence in his conquests: "The people of Al-Hasa are rejectionists and we forced them into Islam by the sword,"[151] he said.

Even his sympathetic chronicler expresses reservations about his "justice," which is characterized, according to Rihani himself, by the "cruelty in social rulings that Wahhabiyyah is famous for."[152] Glubb Pash (the British colonial officer who played an important role in Jordanian history) said that Ibn Saud "used the massacre to subdue his enemies."[153] Ikhwan (the Saudi army of religious zealots) consistently killed all males, including children, but spared the women, who were enslaved.[154] Those who smoked, who wore perfume or ornaments, or who refrained from praying or fasting were flogged. Rihani adds, "How many right [hands] were amputated for small thefts in the early era of this Sultan? And how many heads rolled to the ground for guilty deeds that could have been erased in different times and places by excuses and repentance?"[155] Ibn Saud's representatives either matched his brutality or even exceeded it, especially `Abdullah Bin Al-Jilwi, the ruler of the Shi`ite region of Hasa'. His name "uttered by mothers was sufficient to scare children off."[156] In one day eight heads from the tribe of Bani Murrah rolled on the ground in a public square. Such was the justice of Bin Al-Jilwi.[157]

With his control of Hijaz secure (he declared himself king of Hijaz in 1925), Ibn Saud kept expanding, placing under his control Najd, Hasa, Hijaz, and `Asir. British support was more subtle or indirect; it was in diplomacy, subsidies, ammunition, and weapons.[158] Once the loyal Hashemites' position could not be guaranteed, the loyal Ibn Saud quickly filled the role, and consolation prizes would be arranged for the Hashemites elsewhere. Britain did not want the ambitious and bloody Ibn Saud, with his army of zealous Wahhabi fanatics, to encroach on new Hashemite zones in Iraq or in Jordan. A new treaty with Britain was drafted, which entailed not only Saudi subservience to Britain but also a pledge of Saudi respect for the other British clients in the neighborhood of Arabia.

The story of the rise of Ibn Saud could not be complete without recognizing the role of his army of zealous volunteers. These men formed his religious army: the *mutawwa`ah* and the Ikhwan. The word *mutawwa`ah* sends fear through the hearts of Saudis, especially in Najd, and especially among the foreign visitors and residents of the kingdom who have to deal with being harassed by those people in whose hands is entrusted the application of the strict Wahhabi standards of "morality" and religiosity. *Mutawwa`ah* (literally, those who volunteer in the service of God, originally the word was *mutatawwi`*, which later came to denote those who morally enforce discipline) now refers to the religious police in Saudi Arabia who go around enforcing Wahhabiyyah's strict standards and bans regarding separation of the sexes, women's dress code and behavior, use of alcohol and drugs, and the display of immoral attitudes or non-Wahhabi religious expressions, including non-Wahhabi Muslims' observances, especially among Shi`ites. In the early history of Saudi Arabia, especially before the declaration of the kingdom, the word *mutawwa`ah* referred to the religious advocates (not scholars or clerics) who maintained ritualistic Wahhabi practices, and who were drawn from the ranks of the "sedentary population of the oases of Najd."[159] These religious specialists accepted the imamate of Ibn Saud provided he adhered to the Wahhabi doctrine, and provided they were allowed to play a role in the enforcement of rituals and practices of Islam (as interpreted by `Abdul-Wahab, of course). Ibn Saud was exposed to them from his Kuwait exile days and was brought up on the teachings of those ultra-Wahhabis. They were the champions of the Saudi cause in insisting on collection of *zakat* (almsgiving, one of the five pillars of Islam) and heeding the call for jihad (holy struggle, but here it refers to combat in the cause of the Islamic ruler, in the name of Islam, of course) once issued by Ibn Saud. Ibn Saud was keen on referring to his acts of expansion, plunder, conversion, slavery, and conquest as acts of jihad. He, of course, was not alone in exploiting a term that did not originally have a purely military connotation. He was not the first—and Bin Ladin has not been the last—to rationalize his campaigns of violence and killing by invocation of jihad.

The role of the *mutawwa`ah* later developed into the contemporary body of religious and moral discipline known as the Committee for the Commanding of Virtue and Prohibition of Vice. They still roam the streets with their menacing sticks, the way they did before the creation of the kingdom. They are allowed to threaten and punish because they are obedient servants of the Sauds. They first officially gave Ibn Saud allegiance upon entering Riyadh in 1902, and for that they were rewarded politically and materially. They were also instrumental in forming the fighting force of the nascent Saudi entity.

The Ikhwan (literally, Brethren, which should not be confused with the Muslim Brotherhood of Egypt—also known as Al-Ikhwan Al-Muslimun, an Islamic fundamentalist movement, and the first one of its kind in modern times) refers to the fighting force that Ibn Saud formed in order to quell the threat of rival tribes. They were drawn from the tribal confederations and helped to conquer and then preserve territory under Saud's control. In the classic study of the movement, they are defined as the "Bedouins who accepted the fundamentals of orthodox Islam of the Hanbali school as preached by Abdul-Wahhab which their fathers and forefathers had forgotten or had perverted and who through the persuasion of the religious missionaries and with their material assistance of Abdul-Aziz abandoned their nomadic life to live in the

Hijrah which were built by him for them."[160] Rihani defines them as the "fighting, fanatic, and newly converted religious element in Wahhabiyyah… [They] are the soldiers of `Abdul-`Aziz Ibn Saud who were previously roving nomads, of the ignorant [sic] Bedouins, and they then converted to the religion of *tawhid* and became Muslims. In their extremism, they think that whoever is not one of them is not a Muslim, and they indicate that in their salutation: 'Salaam on you fellow Ikhwan [Brethren], may God salute the Muslims. If a Sunni or a Shi`ite salutes them, they do not salute back.'"[161] Rihani talks about the *mutawwa`ah* as a branch of Ikhwan: they are the ones who teach religion to the masses, while the `*ulama*' teach the *mutawwa`ah* their religion.

The Ikhwan were notorious in the region for their religious fanaticism. The Lebanese poet Bulus Salamah said of them: "They thought hatred and fanaticism are a religion, which religion can survive hatred; oh, you utra-Ikhwan, you have narrowed the religion and deviated from the path of the mainstream; you have only saw in religion repression, hatred, resentment and disdain;…you martyrs of ignorance, how many of an ignorant died for a hollow idea…."[162]

The Ikhwan were the expression of a revivalist movement who wanted to reignite the original `Abdul-Wahab-era intensity of the movement.[163] *Mutawwa`ah* proselytizers roamed Najd, calling on people to settle in encampments known as *hajr* (destination of migration), or even *yathribiyyat* (in reference to Yathrib, later known as Medina of the Prophet after he migrated there from Mecca in 622). For them, this was a haven away from the abode of paganism, and they called themselves Ikhwan after an *ayat* in *Surat Al-`Imran*: "And hold firm, all together, to the rope which Allah stretched for you, and do not be divided amongst yourselves; and remember Allah's favor on you for you were enemies and he joined your hearts in love, and by his Grace you became *ikhwanan* [brethren]...."[164] Ibn Saud would frequently cite this verse upon meeting the Ikhwan. There was inherent conflict in Ibn Saud's relationship with them: they were eager to enforce a strict Wahhabi religious order, and Ibn Saud wanted a kingdom and glory, with less concern for principles. Ibn Saud's ambition extended to the entire Arab world, and he left his friend Amin Rihani with the impression that he wanted to be king of all Arabs.[165] It would have been impossible for him to think that he could unite all Arabs under the banner of Wahhabiyyah.

To obtain the loyalty of the Ikhwan, however, Ibn Saud permitted a rejuvenation of the original Wahhabi fanaticism, including the casual *takfir* (declaration of the infidelity of other Muslims who are not Wahhabi, especially if they happen to be Shi`ites). Senior clerics of Wahhabiyyah declared as early as 1927 that Shiites "should be prohibited from displaying the rituals of their false religion" and that they should be "converted" to Wahhabiyyah, and that those who refuse would be exiled, if not killed.[166] Wahhabis of Ikhwan also invoked the method of *takfir* against other Wahhabis who did not settle in their encampments.[167] The differences between the Ikhwan and Ibn Saud appeared as early as 1925, when he adopted a relatively pragmatic policy in handling the Hijaz; he wanted kingdom and rule and they wanted an opportunity to spread the message of Wahhabiyyah and enforce a strict moral order against the will of the local population. To win his hostile audience in Mecca, which had a tradition of theological teachings that clashed with the strictness and eccentricities of Wahhabiyyah, Ibn Saud—perhaps out of dissimulation— promised self-rule and respect for local traditions. This, for fanatical Ikhwan, was tantamount to toleration of infidelity, and they were not prepared to accept it. Furthermore, Ikhwan wanted to ban travel to infidel countries such as Kuwait and to continue the war against "the pagans." Ibn Saud, out of pragmatism and deference to his British patrons, from whom he was receiving regular bribes—subsidies in diplomatic language—could not go that far. It is in this context that the rebellion of the Ikhwan (1927–30) can be understood.[168]

The Ikhwan raised religious objections to the rule of Saud, objections that reemerged during the 1979 Mecca rebellion, and still later by a wide range of internal Saudi dissidents, from the extremes of Bin Ladin to the more mainstream fundamentalist ones. The Ikhwan objected to Saud's close relationship to Britain, his "serial marriages with daughters of tribal shaykhs, and slaves, and his luxurious lifestyle."[169] The Ikhwan also wanted to "Islamize" the infidel Shi`ites—the brutal rule to which they were subjected was too mild and lenient by their standards. Jihad, as defined by Wahhabi, had to continue and extend beyond the horizons of Najd and Hijaz. They also raised relatively "minor" issues, such as the travel of Ibn Saud's sons to the infidel lands of Egypt and London, and the introduction of the telephone and telegraph in the kingdom. Back in 1920, the most senior cleric, with the support of other senior clerics, had protested the use of the telegraph in the kingdom. These were satanic innovations by their standards,[170] and they frequently cut telephone lines.[171] One member of the Ikhwan once hit a servant of Ibn Saud because he was riding a bicycle. Bicycles in Najd were called "Satan's carriages" and were seen as innovations that operate by Satanic magic.[172] Ibn Saud felt pressured enough to hold a conference and defer to Wahhabi `ulama.' Ibn Saud also destroyed telegraph stations to appease the rebels. The 'ulama' mostly expressed sympathies to the demands of Ikhwan but still recognized the full prerogative of

Ibn Saud in the declaration of jihad and the collection of *zakat* (obligatory almsgiving). They also declared him to be a good Muslim, which was crucial.[173]

After a symbolic threat of resignation, Ibn Saud rallied popular support and gathered the loyal `ulama'` to prepare a counterattack. The role of the `ulama'` was then relegated to ritualistic and purely religious matters, and to affairs of education in the kingdom. The political issues and matters of jihad were entrusted to the hands of the Saudi royal family. This tradition continues to this very day and greatly serves the purpose of the royal family in the face of local Islamist critics and dissidents. Emboldened, Ibn Saud issued a threat to the Ikhwan in which he thundered:

> You Ikhwan, do not you think that you have a great value for us.... Do not think that you have helped us, and that we need you. Your value is in obeying God, and then obeying us, and if you transgressed you become the target of God's wrath. Oh, by God, do not forget that we have slit the throats of the brother, father, and cousin of every one of you, and we did not capture you if it was not for the sword.[174]

With the obedient clerics behind him, Ibn Saud marshaled a fighting force in 1929 and was assisted by the British, who did not hesitate to use the Royal Air Force against the rebels. The rebels fled for their lives into Kuwait and later surrendered to the British, who in turn surrendered them to Ibn Saud. The British had interceded to prevent a wholesale massacre. "From this day onward," declared the king, "we shall live a new life."[175]

With the defeat of the Ikhwan, and the reshuffling of `ulama'` ranks to reward the subservient ones, in September

1932 Ibn Saud felt secure enough to crown himself and declare Saudi Arabia a sovereign kingdom. The House of Saud domesticated Wahhabiyyah and made it a tool of the state. With Islam's heart within its borders, it was important to render the Wahhabi movement a source of its legitimacy and to undermine any religious challenges to royal rule, especially as their lifestyles grew increasingly "sinful." Ibn Saud treated the state as his personal fiefdom: "The state and its countries and lands are to God, and then they are mine."[176] The king placed the constitutional, legislative, judicial, executive, and financial powers in his hands. No constitution needed to be promulgated, he argued, because the state—in theory and claim—respected the Qur'an as its constitution. The king did not neglect the fanatical element of the Wahhabi movement: they were recruited into the new Committee for the Commanding of Virtue and Prohibition of Vice.

The rule of the king was so personal that what could be called a government was in reality no more than a royal court, though it was divided into departments or bureaus that dealt with the affairs of politics, telegraph and code, Najd, gifts and accounting, hospitality and delegation, private royalty, jihad, political communication, private treasury, storage, entourage, royal horses, camels, cars, radio, health within the royal palace, and royal guards.[177]

The king's excessive polygamous marriages, which are explained away as an attempt to consolidate the rule of the new kingdom by creating royal bonds among tribes and families, did in fact contribute to future political problems and create rifts within the very body of the royal family. By his own count, the king married "no fewer than 135 virgins, to say nothing of 'about a hundred' others…though he had come to a decision to limit himself in the future to two new wives a year, which of course meant discarding two of his existing team [sic] at any time to make room for them."[178] This large family inevitably evolved factions and wings, affected the struggle for succession, and split the family along blood, and consequently political, lines.[179] This legacy of Ibn Saud is felt in the composition of the ruling elite in the kingdom and the phenomenon of the Sudayri Seven—the seven sons of Ibn Saud from Hussah Bint As-Sudayri who dominate key positions in the government today.

Saudi scholar Madawi Al-Rasheed notes this aspect of Ibn Saud's life as a point raised by the tribal elders during his lifetime,[180] but she also notes that his son Sa`ud managed to outdo his father by having fifty-three sons and fifty-four daughters.[181] While there may have been political considerations in marrying into the tribes of Banu Khalid, Shammar, `Anizah, `Ajman, Ash-Sha`lan, Ar-Rashid, and Ash-Shaykh (`Abdul-Wahab's descendants), Ibn Saud also, as Al-Rasheed points out, kept a vast number of concubines—literally slaves in those cases—of "African, Circassian, or Yemeni" origins.[182]

For the Saudi opposition—and this category includes not only the fanatical fundamentalist militants but also leftist, Arab nationalist, feminist, Shi`ite, conservative, and liberal groups, organizations, and parties operating inside and outside the kingdom—Ibn Saud was guilty of political and personal corruption. His personal lifestyle and manners of conquest, not to mention his religious bigotry, constitute a long list that plainly prove his lack of moral and political legitimacy. The most famous Saudi dissident before Bin Ladin, Nasir As-Sa`id, compiled public information about the royal family and wrote a book about their history and scandals in an attempt to discredit them. The book is banned in all Arab countries but can be found in most of them,[183] unlike its author, who has been missing since 1979, when Saudi intelligence permanently disappeared him with the assistance of the PLO's Abu Az-Za`im's outfit in Lebanon.

The large size of the royal family has also added to its political problems, as knowledgeable analyst Fahd Al-Qahtani points out in his book on factionalism in the kingdom.[184] The male descendants have become too numerous to control or to manage, and their expenditure and birth-earned salaries have drained the Saudi budget. One of them, Prince Al-Waleed Bin Talal, told the *New York Times* in 2001 that male members of the royal family earn upon their birth an annual salary of $180,000.[185] This, of course, does not include the various preferential treatments and business deals that they receive as a result of their family name. Moreover, the corruption of one member impacts the entire family. The excesses of many of them have undermined the credibility of the religious foundations of the kingdom. And to this very day, it is estimated that the royal family skims as much as 30 to 40 percent of all Saudi oil revenues.[186]

The king used a combination of tribal tradition and personal style to rule over his subjects. He did not think he needed a system of government or a forum for political representation and deliberation. In his own words: "Some claim that freedom characterizes the situation of Europeans, but in reality the glorious Qur'an brought forth absolute brotherhood and equality that no nation ever dreamed of…. We Muslims [run] our affairs according to consultation, and it has a rule, that advice be committed to righteousness."[187] Yet he presided over a *majlis* (council) through which, in theory only, all Saudis could take their grievances directly to the king. They could express dissatisfaction over any aspect of the government, and he would in turn resolve the matter with his wisdom, charm, and decisiveness. Reality was a bit different. This was no desert democracy, as American reporter David Lamb called it. The standards of wealth, power, and prestige that affect, even in Western democracies, the access of the citizens to the government also apply in Saudi Arabia. Those who are received by the king are screened in advance.[188] The king's councils also have a purpose for the political interests of the monarch; they are intended to show the power of the king and his glory. He is supposed to show hospitality and generosity (and generosity was "a political element well used by him"), and to manifest power. He has to be seen acting in his role as king.[189] He has to exude toughness and manliness, and the signs of his sexual prowess are used to spread an image of machismo and vigor, even for an ailing king. In reality, the *majlis*, whether at the royal central level or the local *imarah* (princedom) level, is mainly for show.

During Ibn Saud's time, the cliché of the king being one with the state was quite accurate. He did have a very small number of advisors (his sons Sa`ud and Faysal along with foreign advisors), but he followed his instincts and whims. State treasury was his to dispense as he pleased, and he kept 17 percent of the budget for his own expenditure and 19 percent for "other expenditure," which he also spent as he pleased.[190] At first he received subsidies from the British, but the discovery of oil quickly enriched him and made him more susceptible to the influences and manipulation of Western oil companies.

The first oil concession in the kingdom was signed with a British company in 1923, and a Saudi finance minister signed an agreement with American Standard Oil of California for the meager sum of $250,000.[191] As a gift, the king received a box of California dates (certainly lower in quality than premium Saudi dates).[192] Oil brought great wealth to the royal family and—

from the standpoint of Wahhabiyyah—"infidels" to Muslim lands. The religious zealots knew that the royal family's commitment to Wahhabiyyah would be subordinate to its political and financial interests. Ibn Saud's advisor, Philby, played an important role in guarding those interests, and he enriched himself in the process too. Development was not a priority for the newly wealthy monarch; the first check from oil revenue went to build the Muraba` palace in 1936.[193] Other palaces for him and for the lucky male princes soon followed. The oil also gradually introduced the powerful American political role; the American-dominated Arabian American Oil Company (ARAMCO) soon replaced British influence in the kingdom, and it was "involved in most public works undertaken during the last decade" of the king's life.[194]

The story of ARAMCO is also a story of a new apartheid system in the kingdom. Its oil facilities employed thousands of people (many were Shi`ites, as the eastern region is predominantly Shi`ite), and the workers lived in dirty slums and were rigidly segregated from the "white areas."[195] Eating and drinking facilities were segregated like the old American South. The turnover rate of Arab workers was around 75 percent.[196] Both the government and ARAMCO were fighting common enemies: Arab nationalism, trade unionism, class-consciousness, and socialism/communism. Despite ARAMCO, when the king died in 1953, he left the kingdom and his family in a state of turmoil and instability.

THE RISE OF FAYSAL AND THE SAUDI ARAB ERA

Aside from his father—the founding king, Ibn Saud—King Faysal probably left the biggest mark on the contemporary history of Saudi Arabia and its growing role in regional and international affairs. That Faysal was mentored by his father added to his pedigree and his lore. Faysal was born to Ibn Saud and a descendant of Muhammad Ibn `Abdul-Wahab—Turfah Bint `Abdullah Bin `Abdul-Latif Al Ash-Shaykh. He was the only son of his mother and had one sister, Nurah, who was married to her cousin—no surprise there—Khalid Bin Muhammad Bin `Abdur-Rahman. The power of this small branch of the family draws from the close support it has received from the religious establishment from the beginning—support that helped Faysal in his campaign against his brother Sa`ud, who became the sovereign upon King `Abdul-`Aziz's death. By blood and politics, this group of Ibn Saud's descendants is also aligned with the Sudayri faction—those sons of Ibn Saud from his marriage to Hussah Bint As-Sudayri. One of the wives of Prince Sultan (minister of defense and second in line to be king) is the sister of Faysal's wife, `Iffat.[197]

Faysal had to wait to be king. He had to carefully plot and maneuver to manage the overthrow of his brother King Saud. Saud was the son of Ibn Saud and his wife Wadha' Bint Muhammad Bin Barghash Bin `Aqqab, from the family of `Uray`ir, of the important Banu Khalid tribe. Saud left some fifty-three sons when he died in 1969 but all have been prohibited from public office, though they are allowed to engage in business.[198] The bitterness toward Saud and his rule (from 1953 until his overthrow in 1964) is so intense that he is erased from official records, and his portraits are nowhere to be found in the kingdom. Saud's personal indulgences, sexual and financial, facilitated the efforts of Faysal and his allies. He may not have been allowed to emulate the excesses of his father because he did not have the powers or the shrewdness of his father. There are always stories about him—about his extravagant travels, or the use of twenty-five thousand lightbulbs in the garden of his palace.[199] Faysal's camp relished leaking details of his life to the always-bribable Lebanese press. Ironically, one of his successors, King Fahd, exceeded the indulgences and excesses of Saud, but he was protected from the media, which was instructed to call him "Guardian of the Two Holy Places," perhaps in an attempt to counter his powerful reputation for sin and extravagance. However, accounts favorable to Faysal, even scholarly outputs, also stress Faysal's *aversion* to Saud's corruption.[200]

King Saud lived during the turbulent Arab Cold War years when Nasser of Egypt was fighting bitter media and political wars with the Saudi government—and later a proxy war in Yemen.[201] Nasser's air force even bombed targets on Saudi soil.[202] Unlike his successor, Faysal, Saud bungled badly. He switched sides too many times. Nobody knew where he really stood, or whether he stood for anything. He would pose as a progressive one day and would later be exposed as somebody who botched an assassination attempt on Nasser's life. Seeing him as a weak person, Nasser tried to exploit differences within the royal family to steer things in his favor. He tried unsuccessfully to manipulate Saud, but Faysal's patience had its limits. He could not allow Nasser to interfere in internal Saudi matters.

King Saud was overwhelmed with the administration of the kingdom. He did not have a modern apparatus of power, but he ruled through his close advisors—most of them non-Saudis. A council of ministers was instituted at the end of Ibn Saud's era. Faysal ran the council and Saud saw his power slipping from his hands. Learning from his father, he tried to rule through the informal network of politics. He created a close circle of advisors—also mostly non-Saudis—which included a former Nazi diplomat. His advisors were unable to help solve his financial problems, which were partly exacerbated by his expenses but also burdened by a debt of $200 million left by his father.[203]

In order to stem the influence of his brother, Crown Prince Faysal, the king abolished the position of prime minister, hoping to consolidate power in his own hands. He brought his own people to the administration. Some were forward-looking, like the progressive innovator `Abdullah At-Tariqi. This Egyptian- and American-educated Najdi specialized in petroleum issues and became oil minister in 1960. He was influenced by Arab nationalism and Nasser's ideas. He fought off ARAMCO and may have been the person most responsible for the idea of OPEC (Organization of Petroleum Exporting Countries), which came into being in September 1960.[204] He called for the renegotiation of all Arab petroleum agreements to better reflect Arab economic interests.[205] At-Tariqi wanted OPEC to represent the interests of developing countries, and not the demands of Western markets and governments. At-Tariqi became so outspoken in his liberal, even radical, views that Prince Faysal, who was brought in by Saud to help in managing the affairs of state, dismissed him from the ministry in 1962. After this At-Tariqi had to seek haven in Beirut. He never assumed another political or economic position in the kingdom, although he was allowed to return, silently, to Saudi Arabia in his later years.

Prince Talal was another liberal member of Saud's government. He was a son of Ibn Saud from an Armenian wife (or concubine). He was influenced by Nasser's views on Arab nationalism, although he now tries to downplay that radical period of his life.[206] Like `Abdullah At-Tariqi, Prince Talal was dismissed in 1961. He was proposing the establishment of a consultative council, which Faysal adamantly rejected. He sought refuge in Nasser's Egypt and declared the formation of the Free Princes' Movement—a takeoff on the Free Officers' Movement, which led the Egyptian "revolution" of 1952 against the monarchy. His move was a great bonanza for Nasser's propaganda, and Nasser put it to great use. It was such an embarrassment to the royal family that Talal, once allowed back into the kingdom in the late sixties, had to accept that he would never hold a governmental position. Faysal would never forgive him for what he had done. He now confines his activities to charity work and to membership in the royal family council. Although he spends most of his time outside of Saudi Arabia, he remains a liberal voice for profound political and social reforms within the kingdom but has no impact on royal family politics.

During the 1950s and 1960s, the impact of radical Arab politics on the kingdom was profound. Dissidence took shape in nationalist, socialist, and liberal forms, and the new professional class sought a voice in a country dominated by the elite of the elite of the royal family. Fear of dissent and coups was so intense that the king issued an order in 1956 prohibiting Saudis from traveling abroad for study. Two groups of officers were executed in 1956 and 1958 on grounds of plotting coups.[207] Faysal was worried, and he threatened to use the tribally based National Guard against the king. As a result, the king was forced to abdicate power in 1964, and King Faysal took over.[208] Yet only seventy-two princes out of fifteen hundred were lined up against the king.[209] Al-Qahtani (a far more knowledgeable observer of such matters) counts twenty-six sons of `Abdul-`Aziz, out of thirty-three alive at the time, voting against Saud.[210]

Faysal quickly took control; he ordered a pledge of allegiance from military commanders, and he cloaked his statements with the legitimacy bestowed upon him from the Wahhabi religious establishment that trusted him. He passed over Muhammad (nicknamed the Father of the Two Evils), who simply said: "I am a simple man, I am not a statesman."[211] Muhammad was also remembered for insisting on watching pornographic movies on the *USS Murphy* when accompanying his father to meet President Roosevelt, and for machine-gunning dozens of Ikhwan rebels in 1929, after their surrender.[212] Instead of Muhammad, Faysal designated the pious and nonthreatening Khalid as the crown prince. Prince Sultan was appointed minister of defense and continues to hold that job, which has made him one of the wealthiest and most powerful members of the royal family.

Faysal is considered a reformer, and yet he smashed many of the reform ideas of the technocrats and the liberal princes who were part of Saud's government. The idea of the consultative council was shelved, and the shifting foreign policy of Saud, who fluctuated in his Arab allegiances and alliances, was changed to accommodate a firm alliance with, and reliance on, the United States. Faysal benefited from a flood of oil revenues, and the wealth enabled him to build the infrastructure of the nascent kingdom. In comparison with his father or his troubled and incompetent brother, his rule appears more systematic and stable. However, this is partly due to the fact that King Faysal ruthlessly suppressed dissent, within and outside the royal family, and that he solidified an alliance with the United States and served Western interests in their war against Nasser and Arab nationalism.

His reputation for austerity and asceticism served him well, although famed Saudi dissident Nasir As-Sa`id tells a different story. But As-Sa`id's accounts are not always reliable and can never be verified, and he mixes facts with his obsession with Jewish conspiracies and ancestries. Sa`udi *'ulama'* were brought into the government, but as a subservient arm, and not as an independent edict-issuing body of independent scholars. A ministry of (Islamic) justice was established in 1970 toward that end. Handsomely salaried clerics toed the government line. Faysal and his wife championed education, or so the official story goes, and he was able to push through education for girls despite the objection of clerics. He placed the education of girls directly in the hands of the clerics, thus ensuring that they would only receive rigidly religious indoctrination at the hands of Wahhabiyyah zealots. He also convinced skeptical clerics that technology is acceptable provided it serves a religious purpose. The heavy religious content of Saudi media illustrates this point. Thirty percent of all radio programs are religious, while 25 percent are news programs; the rest cover a combination of culture, sports, and miscellaneous subjects.[213]

The changes that Faysal brought about included an attempt to appear less medieval to the outside world. He abolished slavery in 1962 (although human rights organizations continued to report slavery in the kingdom), promised to spread the message of Islam (more on that later), institutionalized clerical roles in government (to serve the royal family better), and introduced centralized economic planning and five-year cycles. The oil boom revenues allowed the king to buy more political legitimacy by extending a generous "from-the-cradle-to-the-grave" welfare system to the population. Some were awarded more than others, of course. Favored tribal shaykhs, for example, "in Tarabjal and al-Jawf in the north, and Abha and Najran in the south-west, received benefits from state agencies."[214]

In oil policies, Faysal trusted the famous Ahmad Zaki Yamani, and by the admission of the latter, he rewarded him with large swaths of land, which made him a very wealthy person over the years, even after his ouster from the government by King Fahd. Ahmad Zaki Yamani negotiated the Saudi oil policies without antagonizing Western oil companies.[215] Yamani's relationship with Faysal was private and did not go through official government channels. Yamani's orientation in the economic realm was consistent with Faysal's orientation in foreign policy. He succeeded in securing a strong alliance with the United States and cooperated with the United States in its Cold War in the Middle East and beyond. Together, they succeeded in steering OPEC's policies in pro-Western, pro-capitalist directions.

Some oil surplus revenues were deposited in European banks, but most went to U.S. banks. Even when Faysal had to grudgingly join an Arab consensus, as when he joined the 1973 oil embargo to protest U.S. support for Israel in the 1973 Arab-Israeli War, he cooperated with the United States behind the scenes to soften the impact on Western economies. He also used the vast oil revenues at his disposal to pour money into pro-Western regimes in Lebanon and Jordan and to finance military campaigns against leftist and Arab nationalist insurgents in the region.[216] Internally, Faysal was too strong politically to allow for the factionalism within the royal family to affect his rule; the famous Sudayri wing had to wait until after his assassination in 1975 to gather its momentum and start building a power base in the government.

Faysal had a warm relationship with the clerical establishment, although the relationship encountered strain that was caused by the inauguration of Saudi TV in 1965; demonstrators marched to the station to occupy it and were led by Khalid Bin Musa`id (a royal family member and the brother of Faysal Bin Musa`id, who would later assassinate King Faysal). Faysal dealt with the demonstrators the way he always dealt with dissent: brutally and ruthlessly. The minister of interior—the then prince Fahd (later king)—relished the opportunity to teach the enemies a lesson. Even Prince Khalid Bin Musa`id was executed.[217] Those who were lucky enough to be thrown in jail would not be released until after the assassination of King Faysal. To appease the sentiments of the clerics, the king went overboard in utilizing the information and communication systems in the kingdom to send very conservative religious messages. Special Qur'an radio stations were also established. The state cracked down further after the 1969 coup d'etat, in which, according to one source, Prince Talal was implicated.[218] The plotters had intended to declare a "Republic of the Arabian Peninsula."[219] Up to two thousand people were arrested in 1969. Another round of arrests and torture took place the following year, while the minister of interior, Prince Fahd, declared confidently: "The internal situation in Saudi Arabia is perfect."[220] Opposition was not confined to the religious or Najdi elements only or to disgruntled members of the royal family. The spectrum included trends from the far left (communists and socialists) to Arab nationalists (Ba`thists or Nasserists), among others.[221] In the legal realm, the state insisted on its misogynistic practices, refusing to respond to demands for liberalization and openness, putting more restrictions on exogamous marriages, and making it illegal for Saudi women to marry non-Saudis.[222]

Faysal's enmity with Nasser, and his uncompromising hostility toward communism and Judaism (not just to Zionism as a political movement), characterized his aggressive foreign policy in the region. His collision course with Nasser was finalized after the 1962 civil war in Yemen (supported by Egypt and Saudi Arabia on opposite sides),[223] and his assumption to the throne increased his commitment to battle Nasser's influence in the Arab world. He tried, partly at the behest of the United States, to create a regional security alliance aimed against communism and nationalism. Thus was created the international Islamic fundamentalist movement, over which a hue and cry is now raised. It was the brainchild of Faysal and his American benefactors.

The rise of Faysal, in Saudi Arabia and far beyond, was augmented by the death of Nasser in 1970. Prior to that point Nasser had been the most popular and influential Arab leader in the twentieth century, though his power was deeply if not fatally weakened by the 1967 war and the humiliating defeat of his army. Nasser had fiercely attacked Faysal and his camp of right-wing governments and movements. He dubbed them "the reactionary forces" and exposed their relationship with the United States and the West. After the defeat of his army in 1967, his rhetoric drastically softened. His plan for the reconstruction of Egyptian armed forces in preparation for the coming battle with Israel (which came in 1973 at the hands of his successor, Anwar As-Sadat) required a large sum of Arab funding. Saudi Arabia was to be the main source for Egyptian rearmament and development.[224] Faysal met Nasser's demands and convinced other oil-rich Arab governments to do the same, knowing that he was buying Nasser's marginalization in Arab and inter-Arab affairs, and with that, he was also buying political legitimacy for his regime. Faysal also asked for, and received, an Egyptian commitment to withdraw troops from Yemen.

The Saudi king was posing as the leader who came to Nasser's rescue in a moment of need. Pro-Saudi press leaked stories of Faysal exchanging pleasantries with Nasser and of Nasser's praising Faysal. The Arab Cold War came to an end at the Arab summit in Khartum in 1967, when Nasser and Faysal emerged together as new friends and allies. Faysal had won the Arab Cold War, and Nasser was a different Arab leader after that. He watched while King Husayn of Jordan massacred Palestinians (civilians and fighters) in the infamous events of Black September. In fact, Nasser refused to cast blame on King Husayn, who, in his heyday, he had labeled as the "whore king" and "little creation of Western powers."

This inaugurated the new Saudi era, which prevailed in full force after Nasser's death. Anwar Sadat (Nasser's successor) was very close to Saudi intelligence chief Kamal Adham, and he coordinated his policies closely with the Saudis. The United States was pleased with those developments and did not seem to mind the militant ideology and rhetoric of King Faysal. The United States, as will be seen later, was on the side of Islamic fundamentalism in the holy war against communism and Arab nationalism. At the time, Faysal spoke the same militant Islamic language spoken today by Bin Ladin. In a speech he gave in 1969, he stated that "it is a call for jihad for God, for our religion and doctrine, in defense of our holy places and sanctuaries. And I ask God to will for me death, as a martyr for God." But he also, in line with other fanatical fundamentalists, did not miss an opportunity to attack the left: "We have to struggle ourselves to purify [ourselves] from the tumors, and from the corrupt doctrines, and destructive currents."[225] That latter phrase was always a euphemism for leftism.

The Saudi era was characterized by a number of features. First, it underlined the supreme role of Saudi Arabia in inter-Arab politics and the personal role of King Faysal as the guide in the battle against Israel (in his mind it was a battle against Zionism and communism—and he always saw the two as twin evils). Second, the era heralded the emergence of a global Islamic fundamentalist message shaped and driven by Saudi schools and religious centers. It is important to remember that Saudi Arabia was long a haven for disgruntled, expelled, and sought-after Islamic fundamentalists. This was especially the case for members of the Egyptian Muslim Brotherhood—the first and main Islamic fundamentalist organization—who were fleeing Nasser's oppressive rule when he launched a bloody campaign against them after the attempt on his life in 1954. The repression culminated in 1966 with the execution of influential Egyptian fundamentalist intellectual Sayyid Qutb, the martyr-guru of present-day militant Islamic fundamentalists.

Faysal's Saudi Arabia welcomed with open arms the disaffected religious militants, activists, and teachers and put them to a good use. They filled influential spots in key ministries, and they managed and staffed schools and universities. They were the ones who guided the propagation of Saudi Arabia's Islamic message, who harmonized it with a non-Wahhabi (and an anti-Wahhabi) world. Wahhabiyyah, for example, does not belong to any of the four schools of Sunni Islamic jurisprudence. It considers itself to be above them.[226] Later on, the Saudi religious establishment softened that attitude and wanted to be considered part of the ultraconservative Hanbalite school.

Third, the Saudi era was also characterized by an Islamization of the Palestinian cause. One has to remember that the PLO, including Fatah, at the time was adhering to a largely secular message about the Palestinian problem. The Palestinian left played a crucial role in the Palestinian struggle, its political deliberations and discussions in Palestinian political institutions, and in the Arabic press. Saudi Arabia wanted to indoctrinate a religious line that referred to the struggle as jihad, and to *fida'* (a secular term that means sacrifice, a preferred word at the time in reference to Palestinian fighters, who were known as *fida'iyyin*, self-sacrificers) as martyrdom. More than that, the Saudi government wanted to co-opt the Palestinian political movement to undermine the growing role of leftist radicalism. Yasser Arafat, and his right-wing faction within the Fatah movement (the Hasan brothers primarily and Abu Jihad), allowed the Saudi role to be enhanced within the movement in return for millions in Saudi blackmail money. The money allowed them to manipulate the movement, on behalf of the United States, and to spare Saudi territory from any PLO military activities.

Fourth, the Saudi era was characterized by a strong push for a supreme U.S. role as "an honest broker," something that would not have been possible without Saudi intervention with Arab governments, many of which at the time were aligned with the Soviet Union. Saudi Arabia played that role behind the scene to please Washington and to remove the Soviet role from the Middle East. This was very important during Faysal's time, although the Saudi position toward the Soviet Union later softened under Fahd for pragmatic purposes. It also allowed Fahd to better leverage the United States.

At the Arab level, the Saudi era meant a severe setback to progressive opinions and ideas of the enlightenment. Publishing houses, newspapers, and magazines fell under the spell of Saudi money, and that reduced—and in some cases eliminated—critiques of Saudi policy and government, and muzzled progressive viewpoints and analysis. It also pushed for the right-wing reactionary position of the government on social and cultural issues. *Al-Hawadith* magazine, the most widely read magazine in the 1960s and 1970s in the Arab world, was produced by its editor, Salim Al-Lawzi—later assassinated in Beirut—as a mouthpiece for Prince Fahd (later king). Faysal was able to utilize American obsession with the communist threat in the Arab world to launch an international and regional struggle to stem out leftist influences from the ranks of Muslim and Arab students, in the region and around the world. Sadat coordinated with Faysal in his decision to expel Soviet experts from Egypt in 1972, and in his oppressive campaigns against leftist and nationalist presences on college campuses by supporting and unleashing Islamic fundamentalists, who later grew so strong and independent that they (or their offshoots) finally killed him.

Sixth, the Saudi era changed the nature of inter-Arab politics and facilitated the destruction of the rivalries between a "progressive" camp and a "reactionary" camp, which was instituted by Nasser in the late 1950s. The Saudi government succeeded in averting the consolidation of a "progressive" camp after Nasser's death and co-opted Arab nationalist regimes through payoffs and trickery. Saudi Arabia would always deflect criticisms of its pro-American policies by invoking its heavily religious discourse on the Palestinian question.

Seventh, the Saudi era put an end to schemes for unity in the Arab world. Nasser's past experiences, especially with the United Arab Republic (1958–61) between Syria and Egypt, and the ambitious visions of the Socialist Arab Ba`th Party (the pan-Arab party that seized power in coups d'etat in Syria and Iraq in the 1960s), impacted the legitimacy of other Arab regimes. New regimes had to pay tribute to Arab unity and to Arab integration as soon as they assumed power. This was particularly true in the Arab East (*mashriq*). There was a "unity" experiment between Syria, Libya, and Egypt in the early 1970s, but everybody knew that it existed only on paper. With Nasser in power, and with the anticolonial discourse in vogue, the nature of Arab entities (*aqtar*, in reference to individual Arab states that were created by colonial powers, as opposed to the Arab *ummah* [the larger nation, or *volk*], a goal of Arab people) looked transitory. They were a mere phase in the path toward the eradication of the consequences of Western colonial legacy.

Faysal also sought to replace the regional intergovernmental organization that was based on Arab identity (the League of Arab States) with the more religious-oriented Muslim League. The arson attempt on Al-Aqsa mosque in 1969 was a golden opportunity for the Saudi government; Muslim passions were inflamed, and the mood was angry. In 1970 Saudi Arabia convened "twenty-three foreign ministers of Muslim countries...to establish the General Secretariat of the Muslim League under Saudi patronage."[227] Saudi Arabia used the Muslim League and the Islamic Conference to propagate the Saudi message and to propagate the Wahhabi message.[228] The oil boom also allowed Faysal to disperse funds to countries and charities for the political benefit of his regime.

Faysal was assassinated by his nephew Prince Faysal Bin Musa`id Bin `Abdul-`Aziz while waiting to see the Kuwaiti oil minister in March 1975. Less than three hours after the assassination, the Saudi government announced that Faysal Bin Musa`id was mentally ill and "that he did his deed on his own, and nobody had any relationship with what he did;"[229] yet in the wake of the assassination, the Saudi government investigated and arrested fifteen men.[230] The royal family council met and appointed Khalid Bin `Abdul-`Aziz as king, and Prince Fahd was appointed crown prince.[231] The designation of Fahd bypassed the traditional succession advantages of two princes:

Nasir and Sa`d.[232] It was clear then, for Saudis and non-Saudis alike, that the real ruler after Faysal was Fahd.[233] Khalid was a pious man afflicted with heart problems and had little interest in wielding political power. He was a transitional figure, and his appointment would have averted struggle and conflict within the royal family.

The assassination itself and the motives of the assassin(s) remain a mystery. The government continued to insist that the culprit was mentally ill. One cynical Lebanese reporter commented that you have to be truly mentally ill to believe the story of the assassin's mental illness.[234] He was a member of a branch of the family that was historically critical of the royals' senior members. He studied in the United States and switched between schools and universities in California and Colorado. Some in the Saudi press would use his arrest on a marijuana possession charge as "evidence" of his mental illness. Much was made of his lifestyle in America during the free love era. He was certainly political and expressed public criticism of the royal family and its policies.[235] He believed that his family was the biggest obstacle to progress in the Arab world, and maybe that opinion was sufficient to declare him mentally ill. Unfortunately, mental illness is not a defense against the death penalty in Saudi Arabia—or in some U.S. states for that matter—and a few days after assassinating the king, Faysal Bin Musa`id was beheaded. [236] The influence of the Saudi government in the Arabic press at the time can be substantiated by the prompt propagation of the hastily produced official Saudi account of the assassination. Speculation was not not welcomed by the royal family. Arabic newspapers in Lebanon and Egypt competed to provide evidence of his mental illness. An Egyptian newspaper reported that he was once naked in a hotel lobby in Cairo; another one reported that he used to don military uniforms (as an indication of his Napoleonic complexes).237 In the absence of hard evidence and open records in the kingdom, conspiracy theories about the assassination proliferated in the Arab world.

THE FAHD ERA

The new government must have felt some political insecurity after the death of Faysal. The government quickly announced an amnesty of some political prisoners and the promotion of some military officers, although Fahd asserted that the line of King Faysal would continue in the kingdom. Fahd was also appointed first deputy prime minister, and Prince `Abdullah Bin `Abdul-`Aziz (commander of the Republican Guard) was designated second deputy prime minister, which indicated that he would be heir to King Fahd upon his assumption to the throne. Faysal's son, Sa`ud, was appointed foreign minister, and Nayif became minister of interior, a position that King Fahd had held.

The kingdom continued its policy course while Fahd was busy consolidating his power. The phenomenon of the Sudayri Seven took shape—the ruling elite that Fahd and his brothers from Ibn Saud's wife Hussah formed after Fahd's rise to power. The Sudayri family is a branch the Al-Baddarin tribe and has been a stable element of the Saudi state since its inception.238 The family has been tied to the House of Saud since before the creation of the state, and Ibn Saud married three women from the family: Hussah (the mother of Fahd and the Sudayri Seven); Waldah (mother of Sa`d, Musa`id, and `Abdul-Muhsin); and her sister Haya (mother of Badr, `Abdul-Ilah, and `Abdul-Majid).239 King Faysal's first wife (mother of his eldest, `Abdullah) was also a Sudayri, and one of Fahd's wives is (or was—it is not always easy to identify specifically the current wives of the king or princes of the Saudi royal house because they habitually marry, divorce, and remarry) a Sudayri.[240] Many Sudayris occupied high positions in the Saudi government over the years. The Seven Sudayris are a crucial element in the succession path in Saudi Arabia.[241] Fahd's six brothers are Sultan (second deputy prime minister and minister of defense and aviation), Nayif (minister of the interior), Salman (governor of Riyadh), Ahmad (deputy minister of interior), `Abdur-Rahman (deputy minister of defense), and Turki, who was deputy minister of defense until 1978, when he fell out of favor; he then left to live abroad for years. He apparently—and one does not know for sure—disgraced his brother by marrying the sister of Muhammad Al-Fasi.[242] This faction is crucial as the country prepares for the post-Fahd era, knowing that Crown Prince `Abdullah (and his other brothers) are quite old.

King Khalid's era coincided with momentous events: from the Soviet invasion of Afghanistan in 1979, which triggered the Saudi government to throw its lot in full force with U.S. covert operations against the Soviet army, to the Iranian revolution and the subsequent Iran-Iraq war (1980-1988). All that added to the pressures of the kingdom. But nothing was more threatening to the internal balance of power and stability than the 1979 Mecca rebellion.

With the help of between two hundred and four hundred Saudi and non-Saudi followers, in November 1979 Juhayman Ibn Muhammad Al-`Utaybi and Muhammad Ibn `Abdullah Al-Qahtani led a siege of the grand mosque in Mecca. Significantly, Juhayman was born in an Ikhwan settlement, and his grandfather died when the Saudis crushed the Ikhwan rebellion in Sibila in 1929.[243] One of his wives was the sister of his comrade Al-Qahtani, whom he declared to be the *Al-Mahdi Al-Muntadhar*—the awaited rightly guided one. For eighteen years, Juhayman worked in the National Guard. He joined the Islamic University in Medina (which was under the influence of the Egyptian Muslim Brotherhood, whose leaders were brought in by King Faysal in years past) and resigned from the National Guard six years before the uprising. He was a popular poet and was charismatic in his tribe. His followers were mostly students at the Islamic University in Medina.[244] He called for the overthrow of the royal family and denounced their immorality and corruption, which he found fundamentally violated Islamic teachings.[245] This was a highly embarrassing affair for the family, and the minister of interior responded with ruthlessness and brutality. The repression did not end the rebellion. The rebels would not be subdued or killed before December 3, 1979, and with outside French paratroopers' help.

Al-`Utaybi's views can be discerned from writings that he left behind, which were banned by the Saudi government. He was able to combine religious and military knowledge, which he used to great effect in his movement. His fanaticism and his self-righteousness remind one of the Bin Ladin phenomenon, although one does not have a record of Bin Ladin's opinions of Al-`Utaybi and cannot tell for certain whether he influenced his thinking. Bin Ladin was a university student at the time and must have heard of the development and followed it in the news. The reference by `Utaybi to his comrade Al-`Qahtani as the awaited rightly guided one—a messiah of sorts—was utilized by the Saudi government to discredit his religious credentials and moral standing, because the concept is more Shi`ite than Sunni. It was easier for the Saudis to focus on that than to respond to his allegations of corruption and injustice in government and society.

The major speech that Al-`Utaybi delivered contained several demands. First, he called for an end to the Saudi royal rule because "no acclamation to the rule of the House of Saud is possible given that their rule and claim to power are based on oppression and subjugation; and they do not adhere to religion, but in fact destroy it."[246] Second, he called for severing ties with the "Christian governments, especially the U.S., and the expulsion of Christian foreigners who work as teachers, educators, military advisors, consultants, and spies."[247] Third, he called for the elimination of "corruption and deviance in society and the strengthening of the application of Shari`ah [Islamic law] rule, and the condemnation of the government for its disregard of that matter."[248]

The government began an immediate crackdown around the country; scores of people were arrested, and the Saudi media went into overdrive making general accusations, speaking of conspiracies, and reaffirming the Islamic commitments of the government. The government, however, knowing that the use of brutal force would be inevitable for its purposes, needed religious legitimization for all of its actions, no matter how violent. The subservient clerics did not disappoint; five days after the beginning of the siege of the mosque, they issued a fatwa in which they authorized the government to "call on [the rebels] to surrender, and putting the weapons aside, and if they do so, that should be acceptable, and they would be imprisoned until their matter is regarded from the standpoint of Shari`ah. If they refuse [to surrender], it becomes necessary to take all measures to arrest them...."[249] But the task of the royal family was not easy; Al-`Utaybi was apparently known, and he used to debate issues with senior clerics, including Ibn Baz.[250] And just as Bin Ladin is in agreement with the religious establishment in Saudi Arabia over many issues, Al-`Utaybi was in agreement with the religious establishment in the kingdom over many matters, although his espousal of the concept of the messiah was at variance with the dominant Wahhabi doctrine. He, of course, disagreed with the political choices of the clerics.

Al-`Utaybi faulted the royal family more than he faulted the clerics. His criticisms of the clerics centered on their political subservience and their personal cowardice in dealing with the royal family. He specifically singled out Ibn Baz: "that they have selected them [the clerics] from people who cannot see [Ibn Baz was blind] so that they cannot see their vices...."[251] In another letter that he had written, he praised the knowledge of Ibn Baz but criticized him for "not condemning those who violate it [Sunnah, or path of the Prophet], and he cites the violation of the state in many matters but is apologetic about them, and wishes them well, i.e., the House of Saud."[252] Al-`Utaybi's writings, especially his treatise on Sunni caliphate, include strong denunciations of the political system of the kingdom. He stresses that the people do not choose the monarch and the princes, and that the people have no say in government, unlike the early (glorified) phase of Islamic history.[253] And in a direct reference to (then prince) Fahd, Al-`Utaybi reminds his readers that one of the requirements of the ruler is his adherence to religious obligation.[254] Khalid, on the other hand, was known to be keenly religious and "he kept a little green leather-bound Qur'an in one pocket of his *thobe* [garb, or *thawb*] and he referred to it quite frequently, mouthing the verses to himself,"[255] although he did not exercise real political power. Like many of the fanatical militants in the kingdom, Al-`Utaybi faulted the government for not being harsh enough in its treatment of the Shi`ites, insisting that they should be declared infidels and treated accordingly.[256]

The government, despite its willingness to use unconditional and brutal force, did not have an easy time crushing the rebellion. The government described the group that was holed up in the mosque as a gang, but there turned out to be hundreds of people. Soldiers were reluctant to act against fellow Muslims, and they insisted that Ibn Baz issue a fatwa sanctioning their actions. The government dilemma and political crisis did not end when the siege was crushed. For months afterward it had to deal with growing assertiveness and disquiet among the Shi`ite population in the eastern region of the country. The Al-`Utaybi movement signaled a growing trend. Young Saudi-educated men who were brought up on the teachings of Wahhabiyyah could not reconcile their faith with either the corruption of the royal family or the foreign policies of the kingdom that were—and are—in contradiction with the religious codes of Wahhabiyyah. These forces would later produce the likes of Bin Ladin and has deepened the royal family's crisis of legitimacy.

The crisis is also reflected in the dispatch of some twenty thousand National Guard soldiers to the Hasa region to suppress Shi`ite unrest and their celebration of the Shi`ite holy `ashurah season.[257] Al-Rasheed asserts that Saudi discrimination against the Shi`ites does not entirely derive from their Shi`ism but is also related to their socioeconomic history as peasant farmers.[258] While this is only partly true, it does not change the reality of discrimination and contempt faced by Shi`ites in the state and society, and it may disregard the strong theological opposition to Shi`ism on the part of Wahhabiyyah. Oppressed minorities often have their socioeconomic status—

real or imagined, past or present—thrown in their faces, to rationalize that oppression or to accentuate it.

Then there was the Fahd problem. Fahd became a focus of the religious and political opposition's ire at the time of the Iranian revolution and the spread of a militant Islamic ideology that questioned the moral credentials and fortitude of Gulf rulers, and in the wake of the 1979 Mecca uprising. Even the politically quiescent clerics began voicing disapproval. It was not that Fahd's lifestyle had not been known since his youth; European paparazzi caught him in his active days when he toured the casinos and brothels of Europe.[259] His drinking problem was also not a secret; news of it reached the CIA and from there made its way to Western media.[260] The scandalous prince had to deal with an embarrassing rebuke from none other than the most senior cleric in the kingdom, Ibn Baz.

Following an extremely lavish reception for the king in Riyadh, where some 10 billion Saudi riyals were spent—or wasted—Ibn Baz complained to Fahd, saying: "We [the clerics] were aware of the ceremonies surrounding your reception in Riyadh, this does not please God, nor the clerics, and nor the believers.... There are in the kingdom those who need food, medicine, and those are more worthy of funding, than the waste in festivals, receptions, and parties."[261] Ibn Baz also brought up the issue of women's education, objecting to a rumored plan that would transfer control of women's education from clerical management to the ministry of education. The government ceased those plans in response to clerical objections. In 2003, however, the plans were finally implemented, partly in response to a tragedy involving the fanatical religious police allowing school girls to die in a 2002 fire, and partly in response to Western criticism of domestic affairs within the kingdom.

The factions within the royal family were demarcated clearly; Fahd and his brothers against the rest, and Fahd's conflict with his own heir, Crown Prince `Abdullah, commander of the Republican Guard—arm of tribal and domestic security. King Fahd succeeded King Khalid after his death in 1982, although he had been running the affairs of the government prior to that. It must have been embarrassing to King Khalid when Prince Fahd, prior to his ascension to the throne, authored the famous Fahd's Plan of 1981, which was a Saudi initiative to solve the Arab-Israeli conflict on terms agreeable to the United States. It included an implicit recognition of Israel by Arab states, in return for the withdrawal of Israel from the lands it had occupied since 1967.[262] Neither Israel nor the Arabs found the plan to be workable given Israel's rejection of the terms, and the then unwillingness of some Arab parties (including the Palestinians) to come out explicitly in favor of recognition of an ever-expanding state of Israel, especially given that months after the Fahd Plan, Israel launched its devastating 1982 invasion of Lebanon. Furthermore, the Reagan administration was in no hurry to pressure or influence Israel to do anything that it did not wish to do at the time.

King Fahd was also concerned with the changing political environment that he found himself in. The Iranian revolution changed the security map of the region, and Saddam Husayn was the Gulf's favorite respondent to Iranian revolutionary ambition. But the kingdom was also intent on lavish expenditure on its military, even if there was no technological infrastructure to deal with the massive import of arms. Table 4.1 below shows some levels of military expenditure in the kingdom.

This of course coincided with a close strategic relationship between the United States and the Saudi government, espe-

Table 4.1

SAUDI ARMS IMPORTS FROM THE UNITED STATES[263]

Year	Arms Imports (In Millions of U.S. Dollars, 1997 Constant)	Percentage of Total Imports (%)
1987	10,320	39.3
1988	7,710	28.0
1989	7,423	28.8
1990	8,900	31.6
1991	9,968	30.3
1992	9,312	25.2
1993	8,962	29.4
1994	8,143	33.0
1995	10,350	35.6
1996	9,862	34.9
1997	11,600	44.4

cially at the behest of King Fahd and his ally Prince Sultan—the third most senior member, politically, of the royal family (after Fahd and `Abdullah) who modernized its armed forces but without being able to marshal a credible military force. Despite the theoretical power of the Saudi military, the Saudi government has remained dependent on outside powers for its security: Iraq and the United States in the 1980s, and the United States after the 1990 Iraqi invasion of Kuwait. Table 4.2 shows the size and capabilities of Saudi military on paper.

Not only did the arms purchases fail to bolster the Saudi sense of security and enhance its sovereignty, but it also seems that Saudi dependence on outside powers—mainly the United States—for its own protection intensified its crisis. One wonders how Saudi Arabia continued to sign defense agreements with the United States and host thousands of U.S. troops on its territory in 2002 and still spend some 37.1 percent of its

Table 4.2

SIZE CAPABILITIES OF SAUDI MILITARY[264]

Size (Sq. Km)	Population (Thousands)	GDP (Billions)	Military (Billions)
2,149,690	16,948	$136	$17.4

Active Military Manpower	Tanks	Combat Aircraft	Combat Ship
105,500	765	336	43

2002 budget on "defense and security" (75 billion Saudi riyal out of 202 billion Saudi riyal).[265] This is likely to raise more questions than answers, particularly since the Saudi budget has been facing successive budget deficits that have forced the slowing down of the "modernization of the country's infrastructure,"[266] and the reduction of welfare benefits to citizens. Many projects have been halted, and contractors have complained for years of nonpayments.

King Fahd has also invested in a program of collective security, which has been discredited over the years. The king, most probably at the behest of the United States, created the Gulf Cooperation Council (which is reminiscent of Western security alliances and pacts of the 1950s), which included Bahrain, Kuwait, Qatar, the United Arab Emirates, and Oman.[267] The council was intended to coordinate Gulf security arrangements with the American protector in the face of Iranian threats, or fears—founded or unfounded—of Iranian expansionism. The council had an unmistakable political message;

it aimed at the insulation of the Gulf countries from the consequences of the Arab-Israeli conflict and at forging ahead with a regional identity that would be more appealing to the American government. To be sure, the charter spoke of coordination with "Arab and Islamic interests," but this was more in the realm of regional public relations.[268] It would not be an exaggeration to maintain that the creation of the council heralded the marginalization of the League of Arab States (GCC), which had to contend with competing interests and rival ambitions. The GCC was fraught with dissent and divisions. There was the Qatari-Bahraini conflict, and the bitter Qatari-Saudi conflict. Qatar, among others, feared that the council was a vehicle for Saudi dominance in the region.[269] This obstructed plans for joint air defense and a joint rapid deployment force, although some of those arrangements existed on paper. Gulf countries have signed bilateral security agreements with the United States, and all of them are now hosting U.S. troops on their territory. This nullified the existence or credibility of the council.

Fahd focused on external and internal threats alike. His interior minister, Prince Nayif, was given full powers to coordinate the works and intelligence of the security and armed services, including the National Guard, in order to ensure political stability.[270] The personal security of every prince was bolstered—in some cases to the tune of twenty-five bodyguards per prince.[271] The consolidation of the powers of the Sudayri Seven did not smooth relations among the various brothers and the wings of the royal family; but they seemed to succeed in eliminating any rival centers of power within the House of Saud.

The era of King Fahd coincided with the Reagan era in the United States. The two right-wingers got along well—not personally but politically. Fahd's influence, and his interest in augmenting the powers of the Sudayri Seven, meant that he would ignore non-Sudayri members of the royal family, even within his own cabinet, the meetings of which he could rarely attend as he was often abroad staying at his palaces in Morocco, Switzerland, or Spain, among other places. Prince Sa`ud Al-Faysal, the foreign minister, was relegated to diplomatic functions and ceremonial roles, while his nephew Prince Bandar Bin Sultan rose to prominence. Bandar's role was key to the development of U.S.-Saudi relations on a strategic level (more on that later). Bandar was allowed to operate with little regard for the niceties of accountability and division of power within the kingdom, assuming that there ever was such a thing. He would go to China on a secret defense mission, a mission his father (minister of defense) and the king would know about, but which the foreign minister (his cousin and brother-in-law—Bandar is married to King Faysal's daughter) would not.[272]

Fahd was also behind the strong support for Saddam Husayn during the Iran-Iraq war. For purposes of domestic control, the royal family did not want to increase the self-confidence of their own Shi`ite population, which had become increasingly vocal about their opposition to restrictions in their religious practices, and their desire for the elimination of anti-Shi`ite prejudice in official Saudi religious propaganda. The Kuwaiti government had similar calculations; in many ways it can be said that Saddam—as the regional phenomenon with regional ambition—was the creation of the Gulf countries, particularly Kuwait and Saudi Arabia, and their respective propaganda machines. They were the ones who, through their media, and their mediocre palace poets, constructed the features of the Saddam personality cult in the Arab world, which Saddam was keenly interested in promoting beyond Iraq. The Khomeini rhetoric scared the ruling families of the Gulf, and he exposed their weaknesses when he ridiculed their subservience to the United States and their manipulation of local clerics whom he dubbed "Sultan's clerics."[273] Somebody who was riding an unprecedented wave of popular support and acclamation could easily expose the vulnerability of those regimes.

King Fahd, along with other rulers, dealt with those threats by a variety of methods. First, they selected Saddam and his army as their line of defense against possible Iranian military advances or adventurism. They also intervened with Western governments, especially the United States, to improve relations between the Iraqi government and Western powers. Toward that end, Saudi Arabia played a role in reconnecting the Iraqi and American governments during the Reagan years. A special envoy, none other than Donald Rumsfeld, was dispatched to Baghdad to begin the process of rapprochement. Domestically, Saudi Arabia, Kuwait, and Bahrain (all with a substantial Shi`ite population—a majority in the case of Bahrain) all led crackdowns against their dissidents and bolstered their military-security forces. They would regularly announce the discovery of this conspiracy or that and sweep up dissidents in a wave of arrests. Saddam was also brutally persecuting his own Shi`ite population, to the indifference of the Arab and Western worlds, if not to their glee. The Saudi government tried to win over some support by utilizing their vast wealth to buy off opposition groups and co-opt their leaders, and they did exactly that with a major Shi`ite opposition group in the early 1990s.

The Iranian government relished publishing the captured American documents—found shredded and then reconstituted—after the takeover of the U.S. embassy. The documents reveal what people knew: that the United States coordinated its policies closely with the Saudi government and other Gulf governments, and that Gulf oil policies were not formulated without prior consultation with the U.S. government.[274] The Iraqi invasion of Kuwait changed the dynamics of the Gulf Cooperation Council, and Saudi Arabia was pressured by the United States to accept American troops on its territory. King Fahd, true to his history, was far more amenable to the U.S. request than his more skeptical Crown Prince `Abdullah.[275] King Fahd's thinking was revealed in the phone conversation that he held with Shaykh Zayid Bin Sultan An-Nahyan of the United Arab Emirates on June 9, 1990. Iraqi intelligence covertly taped the conversation and later released it in transcript form to embarrass the king. In that conversation, King Fahd (after lengthy pleasantries and wishes of long life and divine blessings exchanged between the two leaders) expressed his desire for peace with Israel and Iran. He said, "By God, we do not wish problems with Israel, and we do not wish problems with Iran."[276] He sounds defensive, and reveals his theory about why other Arabs (and presumably Saudis too) are critical of his government. He tells Shaykh Zayid:

> Oh, you, whose life will be long, we as Gulf governments are target for their jealousy; well, they are jealous of us, but where were they when we were poor, possessing only trees and stones…and when we got some, we did our duty…. Those problems that they [Iraqis] entered into, `Abdul-Nasser entered in it, and could not get out. How could you fight the whole world?… And the Soviet Union began to think and reached what it reached by agreeing with the

Americans.... And Israel, oh you whose life is long,
is now number one, they have 200 nuclear warheads
and 47 atomic bombs, and desperate people....[277]

The king's rule in the 1990s was an attempt to deal with
the consequences of the decision to invite (and retain) U.S.
troops in the kingdom. The alliance between the kingdom and
the United States was strengthened and the region was less
unstable for the Saudi government. They had less reason to
hide their strong attachment to a security arrangement with
the United States. Saddam's government was severely crip-
pled, as were his armed forces. He was allowed by the United
States to keep as much military force as was needed to maintain power. After the death of Khomeini, the Iranian government was more inward-looking. Talk of exporting the
revolution was no longer heard in official government
speeches. The Gulf region was more insulated from the consequences of the Arab-Israeli conflict, and Arafat's close ties to
Saddam, even after his invasion of Kuwait, gave Saudi Arabia
and other Gulf governments an excuse to punish the PLO.
They severely curtailed their financial aid to the Palestinians,
although they continued the fanfare in which they regularly
announced the transfer of funds to the Palestinians (but the
money was a tax imposed on the Palestinians working in Saudi
Arabia). They needed those announcements to pretend that
they were still helping the Palestinian cause. Some Gulf governments even established direct relations with Israel, and
there were reports of secret contacts between Saudi officials
and Israelis. But Saudi Arabia, "guardians" of Islam's holiest
sites, could not go that far—not yet—without an "adequate"
resolution of the Arab-Israeli question.

Among the changes instituted during King Fahd's reign was his decision in 1986 to change his title from King Fahd to Custodian of the Two Holy Mosques. The reason is obvious—an attempt by a king who enjoyed no reputation for piety or asceticism to garner some religious legitimacy. The title of the Saudi rulers did change over the year. The title of king, which was used by the British colonialists when they favored client ruling families, has a negative Qur'anic connotation. It implies arrogance, narcissism, and a sense of self-importance. For religious-minded people in Islam, kingdoms are not abodes of God.

From 1902 to 1915 the preferred title for Ibn Saud was Shaykh or Al-Amir (the prince); from 1915 to 1921 it was changed to Imam (the religious leader; it also was used in the past to refer to the political leader of the religious community). The title of king was first adopted in 1926–27.[278] The king must have felt incredibly provoked by the emergence of Khomeini, with his religious rhetoric and Islamic structure of government. So to emphasize the significance of his new title, the king spent lavishly, or so we were told, to renovate and expand the holy mosques in Mecca and Medina. The king declared, "Spending on the Holy Places will be unlimited with their status in our hearts as Saudis and in the hearts of Muslims throughout the world."[279] But the new title was not enough to spare the king the troubles and challenges that came out of his decision in 1990 to invite U.S. troops to Saudi Arabia to fight Iraqi troops in Kuwait.

The king was faced with religious and political dissent soon after the U.S.-led forces expelled Iraqi troops from Kuwait in 1991. Prior to Operation Desert Storm, Bin Ladin had sought senior members of the royal family—including, by their own admission, Crown Prince Abdullah, Prince Sultan, and Prince

Turki (the head of foreign intelligence)—in order to convince them not to permit U.S. troops on Saudi land. He was turned down, although it was never explained how or why he had such immediate access to senior members of the royal family. Even among more mainstream clerics such as Safar Al-Hawali, opposition to U.S. troops was being expressed.

Safar Al-Hawali is a Saudi-educated religious scholar who reached the position of head of the department of `Aqidah (doctrine) at Umm Al-Qura University in Mecca.[280] Al-Hawali broke ranks with the Saudi regime in September 1990, and he produced pamphlets and recorded speeches that question the very thrust of Saudi foreign policy and its response to the Iraqi invasion of Kuwait.[281] For Al-Hawali, the West poses a more serious threat to Saudi Arabia and Islam than did the Iraqi regime, and he posed a series of questions to Ibn Baz, the linchpin of the Saudi apparatus of religious legitimacy. In those questions, Al-Hawali categorically rejects the decision to invite U.S. troops, and while he opposed Saddam, he was more concerned about the influence and hegemony of the West.[282] Mamoun Fandy, who wrote on the Saudi opposition without being critical of the royal family, believes that Hawali's stance is motivated by fear of foreign domination and not by the classic Islamic fundamentalist passion for restoring an imagined glorious past.[283] Another religious scholar who broke with the regime over the war was Shaykh Salman Al-`Awdah, who taught at Imam Muhammad Ibn Sa`ud University and whose lectures circulated widely after the first Gulf War.[284] Like Al-Hawali, Al-`Awdah rejects the invitation of U.S. troops and blames the decision on the incompetence of the royal family in running the affairs of the kingdom. He focuses more on the faults and shortcomings of the political system. And in addition to the religious critics of the government, the royal family also had to contend with the liberal critics, like the forty-five Saudi women who in November 1990 defiantly took their husbands' cars and drove them in the center of Riyadh to protest the national ban on female driving. The participants, many of whom were university professors, were severely punished: they were called whores in mosques; they were taken to hospitals and tested for semen, alcohol, and drugs; and several lost their jobs and passports. The women received harassing calls at their homes for months, and many were monitored.[285]

What followed later in 1991 was a public and intellectual campaign of requests submitted to the king in the form of petitions. Secular and fundamentalist thinkers and intellectuals openly made demands to the king regarding their desires for reform. The first letter (which contained the demands of liberal reformers, and which included a preamble of fealty and allegiance to the king and his family) requested a consultative assembly, regional councils, and more respect for the rule of law. It also asked for greater participation for women.[286] The consultative assembly mentioned in the petition has been continuously promised to the people of Saudi Arabia since the era of King Faysal. Later in the same year, the religious-minded Islamic fundamentalist thinkers and preachers, including Safar Al-Hawali and Salman Al-`Awdah, submitted their demands for reform, which entailed *more* Islamization of the kingdom and even greater application of Shari`ah laws in society. They also demanded a greater role for the `ulama.[287] The fundamentalist group also submitted a memorandum to Ibn Baz, in which they reiterated their demands for a larger role of the clerics in the work of the government, including in individual ministries, and for introduction of Wahhabi morality in the media and public sphere.[288] Unlike the first liberal petition, this one dealt with foreign policy and called on the government to strengthen the Saudi army to allow the kingdom to engage in jihad, and defend its borders without resorting to seek support from "infidel" troops. When the memorandum to Ibn Baz was leaked to non-Saudi media, the royal family was put in an awkward position, because it could not suppress the news of dissent in its kingdom, something that it had customarily done for decades. This after all has been a government that regularly denied the existence of dissent or even of "differences" or "disputes" in the government.[289] It is also a government that has consistently denied the existence of even "one political prisoner" in its jails.[290] Ibn Baz refused to denounce the content of the memorandum despite pressures from the royal family.[291]

But the government, facing pressures from all sides, could not stay still or wait for pressures to subside as it had in the past—as early as 1975, then prince Fahd had said regarding the formation of a consultative council, "We shall finalize this matter in two months. A new consultative council shall be formed because we want people to partake in responsibility."[292]

Thus, in March 1992, coinciding with "the 10th anniversary of [his] accession,"[293] King Fahd announced a package of internal reforms. It contained three separate elements: a consultative council, the Basic Law of Government, and a law for regional provinces. The consultative council was to include some sixty appointed members (increased to ninety in 1997) and a speaker who would serve a mere advisory role. The king would be under no obligation to accept any of their opinions or suggestions or formulations. The membership in 1997 revealed a preponderance of Western-educated professionals[294] and representation of the regional province (where "Najdis occupied almost 40 per cent of the seats").[295] Clearly, the council was intended for the liberal-oriented professional elite.

The members were chosen, according to a hagiographer of King Fahd, because "they [had] proved themselves to be responsible and loyal citizens of the Kingdom."[296] He forgot to add that they were chosen because, among several other factors, they were males; females were excluded from membership in the council, although there has been a debate in the kingdom as to whether women can attend sessions of the council. Members of the council who wish to speak during a session must make their request in writing (Article 15). This council was not intended as a boisterous deliberative body, of course. The Saudi government is now pushing to have the consultative council represented in the International Parliamentary Union. It is certain that the request will be met with approval from a union that in the past accepted representation from such countries as Saddam's Iraq and the communist countries of Eastern Europe.

The second element in Fahd's package of reform entails what is referred to as the Basic Law of Government. Saudi Arabia is one of a handful of countries around the world that does not have a written constitution. It would be impossible for the Wahhabi clerical establishment to accept a written, human-made constitution in a country that has claimed, since its inception, that it lives only by God's words. The Qur'an, the Saudis assert, establishes the constitution of the kingdom. The Basic Law of Government was only intended to draw the basic framework of government in the kingdom and to put on paper the general—very general—boundaries of rights and duties of citizens. Again, the Basic Law was an attempt at reform intended to please the liberal reformers within and outside the royal family and to appease Western public opinion, press, and governments, but without being an actual constitution. Not that Western governments would have made a cause célèbre out of the lack of human rights and rule of law in the kingdom, but the Saudi government became more deeply aware that it was facing very negative images of its style of government and lifestyle in many Western countries.

Lest anybody think the Basic Law is the constitution of the kingdom, note that its first article clearly states that "the kingdom of Saudi Arabia is a sovereign Arab Islamic state with Islam as its religion; God's Book and the Sunnah of His Prophet, God's prayers and peace be upon him, are its constitution." (Article 1.) And the king did not suffer any loss of power from the promulgation of those so-called reforms. In fact, the king remains supreme and may have been able to institutionalize his omnipotent powers in writing. Most articles of the Basic Law in fact grant him sweeping power in all facets of politics and society. The king selects and dismisses the crown prince (Article 5); he presides over the legislative, executive, and judicial branches of the government (Article 44); he is responsible for the appointment and dismissal of judges, and for the implementation of judicial rulings (Articles 50 and 52); he presides over the Council of Ministers, and appoints and dismisses ministers (Articles 56 and 57); he appoints the members of the *shura* consultative council; he approves and amends international treaties, agreements, and regulations (Article 70); he announces the budget (Article 76); and he can amend the Basic Law (Article 83).[297]

And the Basic Law contains language reminiscent of the political language common in the feudal era of medieval Europe. Article 6 stipulates that "citizens are to pay allegiance to the King in accordance with the Holy Qur'an and the tradition of the Prophet, in submission and obedience, in times of ease and difficulty, fortune and adversity." Article 7 claims, with little modesty, that the government in Saudi Arabia "derives power from the Holy Qur'an and the Prophet's tradition." What is interesting about Article 6 is that it is based on a bogus claim; nowhere does the Qur'an urge believers to obey and submit to the king—any king. This is especially true in a religion where submission (which is contained in the very word *islam*) is supposed to be to God only. Article 7's phraseology is from the language of the era of divine rights in medieval Europe. There are many references to God and the Qur'an in the Basic Law; it's as if the royal family were trying to deflect any criticism from people who believe the kingdom is not bound to the Qur'an as a constitution. And the Basic Law (Article 14) specifically states that "all God's bestowed wealth, be it under the ground, on the surface or in national territorial waters, in the land or maritime domains under the state's control, are the property of the state as defined by law." But the article does not say that there is a conflation in Saudi Arabia between the state and the royal family. This article was intended to ascertain the House of Saud's fundamental right to control the oil wealth of Saudi Arabia and to do with it what it wishes.

This explains the vast wealth that some members of the royal family have. The Saudi media do not talk about such matters, and one can follow them only in the Western press, based on estimates. King Fahd's personal wealth is estimated to be around $45 billion (*Forbes* magazine's estimate is $20 billion[298])—but nobody knows for sure, given the royals' secrecy in such matters—which is partly accumulated by diverting some 1,000,000 barrels a day to be sold in the open markets.[299] A system of bribery and kickbacks also brings in more money to the royals. According to an oft-repeated story, his favorite son, the powerful Prince `Abdul-`Aziz Bin Fahd, never leaves his side because a soothsayer once warned Fahd

not to travel without him. Even when `Abdul-`Aziz was still
only a toddler, Fahd would bring him to meetings with heads
of state, and when the boy reached the age of fourteen, he
reportedly received a lump sum of some $300 million from
his father.[300] `Abdul-`Aziz's wealth is estimated to be around
$15 billion. There are regular stories of millions (and even
billions) transferred from King Fahd's account to `Abdul-
`Aziz's account. Yet we do not know for sure the extent to
which King Fahd's wealth is mixed in with the wealth of the
kingdom.

The Basic Law also expounds upon the role of the family in
society, according to the teachings of Islam; and it specifies
that the role of the state is to "protect Islam" and to preserve
the holy places.[301] It contains articles regarding the role of the
consultative council, giving the king, yet again, the supreme
right in its formation and dissolution.

The third element of the reform package refers to local governance. It specifies the powers of the local amirs in each of
the governorates and gives the interior minister overwhelm-
ing powers over local administrations and administrators.
These changes were also intended—in theory—to curb the
tide of widespread corruption around the kingdom. But the
Basic Law and the reforms in general leave many important
questions unanswered. The reality of royal deliberations was
kept a state secret. Citizens are not told how kings are chosen,
or how senior princes are so designated. More important, the
Basic Law has no articles referring to the duties of the king.
There are no provisions, for example, for the abdication or dismissal of the king, not even in the case of physical incapaci-
tation or mental illness.[302]

But none of these elements of reform changed the reality
of politics in Saudi Arabia; these so-called reforms came at a

time when the Saudi royal family felt that it was compelled to take action, to deflect some of the internal and international criticism. And as Madawi Al-Rasheed observes, the announcement of reforms was accompanied by an enhancement of the role of the security-intelligence apparatus in the kingdom, that is, a campaign of harassment, intimidation, and oppression. Vocal critics Al-Hawali and `Awdah were both arrested,[303] among hundreds of others, though no one ever knows exact numbers in a closed and secretive society like Saudi Arabia. Prince Nayif, the interior minister, stated that those who were arrested engaged in "actions that undermined national security."[304] An intense pro-Saudi campaign was launched to praise the royal family and denounce its critics.

With Saddam's Iraq weakened and Iran restrained, King Fahd navigated his kingdom's policies in a more favorable regional environment. The U.S. policy of double containment suited the royal family, and there were some ten thousand U.S. troops on hand in the kingdom just in case they were needed. The dynamics of the government, however, changed in 1995 when the king suffered a stroke, which left him largely incapacitated. The government has since been run by Crown Prince `Abdullah, the heir to the throne, although there is still a hidden role for one of the wives of King Fadh and his son `Abdul-`Aziz (more on that later).

Not much is known about the life and history of `Abdullah. Even his age is uncertain, although he is thought to have been born around 1927, or even earlier. Crown Prince `Abdullah, like many—if not all—of his brothers in the kingdom, is a barely literate individual who has risen within the royal family through his control over the National Guard, which has been used for purposes of internal security and domestic oppression. `Abdullah, as a half-brother of King Fahd, is sep-

arate and apart from the aforementioned Sudayri Seven, and
has charted, until recently, a separate political line. One of
his many wives is—or was—Syrian and is related to the family of Hafidh Al-Asad through his brother. Abdullah has developed a relatively good reputation within the kingdom; he is
not known to be as flagrantly corrupt as Prince Sultan or King
Fahd. For the reformers, he has emerged as a champion simply because he stands outside of the Sudayri Seven (it should
be noted that one of the Sudayri Seven, Prince Salman, governor of Riyadh, is popular and is seen as intelligent and com-
petent, unlike his brothers). He is also praised for his forthright
manner. For not being Fahd, and for not living his earlier life
like Fahd, `Abdullah wins points from the Saudi public.
`Abdullah has also managed to fashion for himself a quasi-
independent foreign policy.

Within the kingdom, `Abdullah was identified with a pro-
Arab nationalist line and was far more reserved, again until
recently, with the alliance with the Americans. He was far
more cautious than his brother about the invitation of U.S.
troops in 1990, and at the meeting with the U.S. delegation at
the time, he was heard saying "by God they will never
leave."[305] `Abdullah had established very good relations with
Arab leaders over the years, especially with the Syrian president Hafidh Al-Asad, which helped his "nationalist" credentials within the kingdom. `Abdullah has also played a role in
meditating between "radical" and "moderate" Arab governments: he was often dispatched by King Fahd to smooth relations with Syria and to prod Syria to be more cooperative in
matters of regional Arab politics. His ties with the Syrian government (and with the ruling of Al-Asad family in Damascus)
enhanced his Arab nationalist credentials in Saudi Arabia, and
in the Arab world.

September 11 and its aftermath has forced the hand of the crown prince—a subject to be explored in greater detail in chapter eight. But suffice it to say that he could not allow his views or opinions to affect his country's response to U.S. pressures; the royal family was more concerned about losing its own strategic and political preferential position with Washington. Before September 11 he was probably determined to pressure his American ally on the Palestinian question and had postponed a visit to the United States. But after September 11 he has acted with the same deference toward the American president that is usually expected from King Fahd. To be sure, he sometimes tries to act independently, as when he visited Russia in September 2003 and praised Russia for its early recognition of the Saudi state.[306] This was the first visit by such a high dignitary of the Saudi state since its creation. But Russia no longer adheres to the communist ideology that the House of Saud so bitterly abhors. There were other reasons for the visit. One Russian newspaper speculated that `Abdullah wants to strengthen ties with Moscow out of fear of further U.S. plans for regime change in the Middle East.[307]

In Arab affairs, the crown prince has not changed the established course, although Saudi Arabia's influence seems to be reduced, perhaps because other Gulf countries have now established close bilateral relations with the United States, and the GCC as a vehicle for Saudi hegemony has been marginalized. Saudi Arabia sat down and watched nervously as Qatar and Bahrain succeeded in forging closer ties with Washington. The crown prince also revealed his political awkwardness and defensiveness in March 2003, during an Arab summit meeting in Egypt, when he berated—in vulgar language—the Libyan leader Qadhdhafi for remarks he made and which the crown prince (mis)interpreted as insults to the kingdom. The scene was carried live on TV, before it was abruptly cut off. Al-Jazeera (the Qatari-based TV satellite station that carries—subtly or blatantly—the political inclinations of the Qatari royal family) ran with it and seemed to find rerunning it to be quite useful for viewers. The stutter of the crown prince, and his loss for words, did not present him in a good light to millions of Al-Jazeera viewers. In the Gulf region, the pace of political reforms in Qatar and Bahrain (and even the United Arab Emirates and Oman) has only underlined the anachronistic nature of Saudi politics, in the eyes of the people of the region and in the eyes of the Western press.

Where the reforms of King Fahd of 1992 were triggered by internal developments and the succession of petitions and demands by sectors within Saudi society, Crown Prince `Abdullah's reforms have been triggered by outside pressures following 9-11, and the terrorist attacks in Riyadh in Saudi Arabia in 2003—bombings of predominantly Western (and Arab) residential complexes that exposed the operation of Al-Qa`idah in Saudi Arabia, something that the kingdom had been denying ever since 9-11. More than any of the early leaders of Saudi Arabia, the crown prince has had to contend with the domestic and international constituency and pressures, without alienating one at the expense of another. And `Abdullah's reforms have been rather piecemeal and incoherent. It is not clear that he has formulated a plan and is acting accordingly. In fact, it is almost certain that he is acting defensively, and one step at a time.

His "reforms" have included the demand that clerics avoid extremes in their religious sermons. There are now constant warnings against ultraextremism (or excessiveness, *ghuluww*) and a promotion of *wasatiyyah* (literally, centrism, but here means moderation) in the propagation of the faith. Toward that end, the Supreme International Council of Mosques, which falls under Saudi influence and patronage, issued the Mecca declaration in September 2003, in which it sought to combat "the deviationist thought, in clear reference to the extremist ideology of Bin Ladin and similar militants." It also warned preachers against falling for the "hard-line interpretations" of the purpose of Islamic laws. And in typical Saudi fashion, and as if to cover the purpose of the declaration, the final statement did not forget to mention the Palestinian cause and to condemn Israeli actions.[308] And as was mentioned earlier, the Saudi government also took gradual steps to respond to the demands for change coming from liberal sectors in the kingdom and from the U.S. Congress. The White House, under administration after administration, has never publicly questioned Saudi policies and has always allowed the Saudi government to proceed in its "reforms" as it pleases. When the White House applies pressure on the Saudis, it does so in private lest it embarrass its valuable ally. Even in March 2004, after the Saudis arrested liberal reformers, and after a Department of State statement that expressed "disappointment" over the arrests, Secretary of State Colin Powell assured the Saudi leaders that the countries' relations remained "quite strong" and free of tension.[309] Saudi leaders know that they can always get away with their pattern of human rights violations and that American leaders would do their utmost to shield them from public and press criticisms.

The reforms that have been enacted center mostly on the promotion of moderation in religious indoctrination. But this is foolhardy at best. How can the Saudi government in response to Western criticisms suddenly nullify the decades-old values and themes that have been at the core of Saudi curricula at all levels of education? And the media scrutiny of sections of the

American press and conservative think tanks, particularly those that are close to the Israeli government, only bring about a constant supply of embarrassing facts and realities: from the language of religious sermons to materials from Saudi textbooks.[310] One day the Saudi government announces the expulsion of some preachers; another day it announces, or it leaks to a newspaper the news, that it will shift responsibility of female education from the clerical establishment to the ministry of education. There is no evidence of a coherent policy espoused by the crown prince. The crown prince, in addition to worrying about the domestic and international pressures, also has to contend with the succession struggle going on within the higher echelons of the royal family.

The crown prince, and the royal family in general, want to stay in power and be able to do what they have done for decades: maintain a close alliance with the United States without having to pay a heavy domestic price. They also have to adhere in some form to the doctrine of Wahhabiyyah, without which the government loses its ruling ideology and falls prey to the attacks of the powerful clerics. The dilemma of the royals has deepened since 9-11 because the kingdom cannot now set its own pace and proceed according to its own timetable. More than at any other time in history, the House of Saud has to respond to developments not of its own making, and sometimes in response to homegrown violence and terrorism. The ruling dynasty's ongoing struggle of succession will have to fashion one formula, or contending formulas, to deal with the pressing challenges.

While the succession path has not been charted yet in Saudi Arabia and cannot be officially charted as long as King Fahd remains alive, it is reasonable is assume that factions are forming and that competition is raging within the family council. One is not privy to the internal deliberations within the ruling family, but one can expect the Sudayri Seven to be lining up in preparation for the day that King Fahd dies. It was noteworthy that when King Fahd went on his regular vacations to his palace in Spain (built as a larger version of the White House), both Prince Sultan and Prince Salman accompanied him, in addition to the ever-ubiquitous Prince `Abdul-`Aziz Bin Fahd, the favored son of Fahd who has been playing an ever-expanding role in government and now holds a cabinet post. The crown prince relies on a different policy team than Fahd and has marginalized the influence of Prince Bandar, while enhancing the powers of Prince Sa`ud Al-Faysal, the foreign minister, who was largely ignored by King Fahd.

Succession for `Abdullah also has to be affected by blood conditions and kin; `Abdullah, unlike Fahd, does not have full brothers and must "make alliances"[311] and form factions away from the dominant Sudayri Seven. Simon Henderson makes reference to Prince Badr (`Abdullah's deputy at the National Guard and his half-brother) as a possible choice for an ally,[312] but that is highly unlikely given the background of Prince Badr as one of the former "liberal princes." It is not easy to speculate on this matter because one does not know anything about the internal dynamics of the royal family, and the choice will be drawn from the ranks of Ibn Saud's sons—and the era of the younger princes (the second generation, or the grandsons of Ibn Saud) has yet to arrive. To be sure, the younger princes will play a role in the formation of factions and the building of networks around the kingdom. Prince Sa`ud Al-Faysal (and his brothers) may be part of `Abdullah's faction, but not all of them carry the same weight, and Sa`ud is debilitated by Parkinson's disease.[313] Prince Turki, the former head of foreign intelligence (Al-Istikhabarat) who mysteriously quit his job days before September 11, will be difficult to deal with by the American government, given all the publicity about his links to the networks of Islamic fundamentalists, which included, by his own admission, Bin Ladin himself. And he still seems to remember Bin Ladin rather fondly. In his own words, "At first he [Bin Ladin] seemed shy, friendly, almost gentle. He was soft-spoken, a man of sparse sentences. Our first meeting must have taken place around 1984, and the last one in 1989 or 1990.... His presence, dignified and reserved, must have made an impression on the Afghans back then."[314] Prince Turki's appointment as ambassador to the UK was not without controversy in the British press, and his chances of rising beyond the rank of minister are rather slim.

It is not unlikely that `Abdullah will settle for serving as king when Fahd dies and will not interfere in the selection of his successor, who, according to the previously charted ranking, will be Prince Sultan. `Abdullah may allow the Sudayri Seven to prevail without a fight, especially as they are the faction with the closest ties to Washington, D.C., the quarter that Riyadh now seems to care about the most. It should also be mentioned that the United States, with its heavy military presence in the region—despite an announced withdrawal of U.S. troops from the kingdom in 2003 and the preservation of "U.S. advisors," and its ties to various branches of the royal family, will not be a mere bystander as far as the succession process or struggle is concerned. The American government will make its preferences clear, especially if—hypothetically speaking—somebody like Prince Nayif, the minister of interior, who is not a favorite among the U.S. security agencies, is advanced to a higher position.

Crown Prince `Abdullah, or the next king, will also have to tackle the serious economic problems facing the kingdom.

Saudi dependency on oil has not changed: the oil sector still accounts for some 75 percent of budget revenues,[315] and the fluctuations in oil prices affect the government's economic policies, especially when Saudi Arabia's economy is (in theory) set by five-year plans. An IMF review of the Saudi economy found a pattern of budget deficits and accumulation of debt that now stands at around $170 billion."[316] By one estimate, "the per capita GDP was worse in 1999 than it was in 1965 before the massive rise in the price of oil."[317] And the recent increase in oil prices is unlikely to relieve the country's problems, because expenditure seems to always exceed predictions. And for the first time, the government, in the voice of none other than Crown Prince `Abdullah, is now admitting that there is a poverty problem in the kingdom. Of course, the timing of the announcement was not innocent, as the crown prince was urging charity to be directed locally, in order to allay U.S. fears of Saudi Arabia funding terrorist organizations. Unemployment has forced the government to restrict those jobs that are available for foreign workers, but there seems to be no solution to this pressing problem. There are some fears that the flow of Iraqi oil may also push oil prices down, thereby harming the Saudi economy further. And then the Saudi royals have to decide what to do with their global Islamic propaganda outlets and organizations, all of which have come under scrutiny from the U.S. Congress. But these serve the government's religious commitment and thus continue to serve as a source of legitimacy. The subject of this global network will be dealt with in the following chapter.

FIVE

Saudi Globalization of Da`wah After the Oil Boom

Islam is a global religion that penetrates borders, assimilates with local cultures, travels to remote regions, crisscrosses continents, and unifies a coherent message suitable, in its eyes, for all of humanity. There is no nationalism in Islam; the religion is intended to serve all people, and it—in theory— recognizes no distinctions of race or ethnicity, preaching that rewards and punishment are on the basis of an "atom's worth" of goodness or evil, as the Qur'an says.[318] Islam was bound to clash with territorial nationalism because its scope is not limited to one piece of land, although Arabs have often interpreted a verse in the Qur'an ("and you have been the best peoples evolved for humankind"[319]) to imply their ethnic superiority over other peoples, perhaps because the Prophet was Arab and the Qur'an was revealed, according to Muslims, by God in the Arabic tongue.

The new revenues of the oil boom—crude oil prices skyrocketed from around $3 per barrel in 1970 to more than $35 in 1980[320]—placed at the disposal of the ruling family huge amounts of money that were utilized to consolidate state power and to expand state welfare benefits and programs throughout the kingdom. It was also used, as was said earlier, to enhance the regional position of the kingdom by influencing the behavior of other states through financial aid. All this coincided with the era of King Khalid, the puritanical Wahhabi, and the hedonist King Fahd. That Fahd's lifestyle did not adhere to Wahhabi standards, or even to the standards of any recognized religion, did not diminish the impetus for state control and propagation of *Da`wah* (Islamic call, or the effort to win converts and adherents). Fahd, knowing that he lacked any religio-moral credentials or virtues, had to zealously support the global propagation of Wahhabi Islam in order to enhance his stature with the religious establishment, vis-à-vis domestic opinion in general. King Khalid did not need to be convinced. He was a true believer. Fahd had another reason to throw money into globalizing Islamic propaganda: his close association with the United States and his increased involvement in U.S. covert operations around the world required Islamic steps on behalf of the kingdom to offset the Western orientations of the kingdom's foreign policies.

The Islamic revolution in Iran also created a rival voice speaking on behalf of Muslims worldwide, especially when Ayatollah Khomeini was preaching the export and spread of fundamentalist revolution. And while the revolution was Shi`ite in sectarian affiliation, it succeeded in inspiring religious advocates and in triggering religious organizations throughout the region. Khomeini also presented a model of revolutionary Islam, in contrast to the conservative model of the House of Saud. He also spent a good deal of time in his propaganda to discredit what he called "the Sultan's clerics" (in reference to those clerics who are subservient to their conservative governments) and to denounce those Muslim governments that are loyal to U.S. interests.

Efforts to globally proselytize the Saudi strain of Wahhabi Islam had begun earlier, in 1962, with the creation of the Muslim World League. The charter of the League states that its goal is to "fulfill God's obligation by propagating his message and spreading it all around the world"[321] and to "unify the word of Muslims."[322] But this was not an easy task: Saudi policies had contradictory contents. How could the Saudi government unify the word of Muslims when it adhered to a small and unrepresentative sect in Islam that is by its very nature highly judgmental and divisive among fellow Muslims and non-Muslims alike? And how could the Saudi government think that it could lead the world's Muslims, the majority of whom are highly critical of the United States, while being so closely associated—militarily and politically—with the United States? And if Saudi Arabia was to succeed in winning over other Muslims, it had to shed the historical image of Wahhabi's imposition of doctrine by way of the sword. To be sure, the global efforts of Saudi propaganda were consistent with Wahhabiyyah doctrine, because according to Wahhabiyyah teachings, "converting" other Muslims, even by force, is good for Islam and good for those who are being converted, because their previous Islam is akin to paganism.

Those efforts can be seen as signs of political and moral insecurity. The Saudi government had to do something in the face of Iranian challenge and in the face of internal challenge to its authority after the 1979 Mecca rebellion. One can see the increase in the size of Saudi financial aid in Table 5.1.

One also sees this pattern of dramatic increases in expenditure in funding of religious propagandists and Qur'an memorizers, as seen in Table 5.2. The drastic increases in funding for U.S. activities can be seen in Table 5.3.

And this increase in expenditure on religious propaganda took place under certain financial constraints during the period, which included decline of oil prices, expenditure on covert operations in Afghanistan and Latin America (and prob-

Year	Arms Imports (In Millions of U.S. Dollars, 1997 Constant)	Percentage of Total Imports (%)
1987	10,320	39.3
1988	7,710	28.0
1989	7,423	28.8
1990	8,900	31.6
1991	9,968	30.3
1992	9,312	25.2
1993	8,962	29.4
1994	8,143	33.0
1995	10,350	35.6
1996	9,862	34.9
1997	11,600	44.4

Table 5.2

FUNDING FOR PRO-SAUDI RELIGIOUS PROPAGANDISTS
AND QUR'AN MEMORIZERS (ARAB COUNTRIES)[324]

Amount (in Saudi Riyals)	Year
798,000	1980
4,526,000	1982
671,000	1985

Table 5.3

FUNDING FOR PRO-SAUDI RELIGIOUS
PROPAGANDISTS AND QUR'AN MEMORIZERS
(IN THE UNITED STATES)[325]

Amount (in Saudi Riyals)	Year
1,304,000	1981
2,321,000	1982
2,418,000	1983
2,198,000	1984
2,477,000	1985

Table 5.4

FUNDING FOR PRO-SAUDI RELIGIOUS
PROPAGANDISTS AND QUR'AN
MEMORIZERS (IN ASIA)[326]

Amount (in Saudi Riyals)	Year
501,000	1980
3,236,000	1985

ably elsewhere), huge expenditure on arms sales, and funding
in support of Saddam Husayn's side in the Iran-Iraq war. The
same pattern of funding priorities is evident in the works of
the Al-Haramain Foundation, which recently came under
scrutiny by the U.S. government for suspicions of ties to terrorism.[328] In 2004 the Saudi government announced that the
Foundation's activities would henceforth be confined to Saudi

Table 5.5

TOTAL FUNDING FOR PRO-SAUDI RELIGIOUS
PROPAGANDISTS AND QUR'AN MEMORIZERS
(WORLDWIDE)[327]

Total Expenditure (in Saudi Riyals)	Year
2,378,000	1975
4,175,000	1977
9,270,000	1978
20,492,000	1980
25,655,000	1983

Arabia itself. Al-Haramain, ostensibly a charitable foundation, spent much of its budget on religious propaganda on behalf of the Wahhabi Saudi government. In its 2003 annual fiscal report, the foundation stated that 35 percent of its expenditure for that year was devoted to "religious propagation and education" and a mere 14 percent was devoted to relief works.[329]

Saudi Arabia, as a government and as a center for unpopular Wahhabi Islam, invested in its religious propaganda in part to cover King Fahd's weak moral credentials and reputation for indulgences in "sins." Unless one considered the former Taliban government in Afghanistan a successful model, the Saudi government failed miserably in winning converts to Wahhabiyyah. Mullah `Umar and other Taliban colleagues were clearly influenced by Wahhabiyyah teachings, knowing that Saudi Arabia sunk millions of dollars into the religious schools in Pakistan during the Afghanistan war. The Taliban government's destruction of the Buddhist statues in Bamiyan in 2000 had the Wahhabi signature all over it. Those statues, after all, survived centuries of Islamic history, which certainly included some intolerant and dogmatic periods, but perhaps none as strict in theological interpretation as the Wahhabis.

By and large, one can say that the Saudi government's global propaganda mission has failed, particularly in winning over the hearts of Muslims worldwide. To be sure, they bought and constructed mosques around the world and co-opted their preachers. They also subsidized publishing houses and prevented the dissemination of anti-Wahhabi writings that could find their outlet in exile and underground publishing houses in the Middle East and Europe, and in the Shi`ite religious literature that has historically been very concerned about Wahhabi dangers to its faith. They bought Arab media outlets and established new ones; they subsidized mullahs and founded loyal religious schools, and they financed a prolific amount of anti-Shi`ite propaganda.[330] But the ideology and even the doctrine of Wahhabiyyah are in deep crisis.

Wahhabiyyah's true believers are in crisis over the hypocrisy of Saudi Arabia's political leaders. Those who are raised on and believe in Wahhabi teachings cannot be satisfied with the state of affairs within the kingdom. The notorious lifestyles, corruption, and even foreign policies of some members of the ruling family are in direct opposition to the principles of the faith. Among liberals, the Wahhabi doctrine is repulsive in its strict puritanical nature and its unending list of constraints, taboos, and punishments. Among most believing Muslims, Wahhabiyyah is embarrassingly extremist and fanatical. By virtue of the compulsory nature of religious indoctrination in Saudi Arabia, Wahhabiyyah has remained, for the most part, a local phenomenon concentrated in the kingdom. Its uncompromising and dogmatic theology, especially regarding women—as will be seen in the following chapter—has made it difficult, if not impossible, to adapt its doctrine to the world's Muslims who are accustomed to a more flexible and tolerant Islam.

SIX

The Question of Women

Saudi Arabia—like Afghanistan—has become a stigmatic symbol for the plight of Muslim women. Women's issues in the Middle East have served as an effective propaganda tool for advancing Western interests—interests that often amount to domination. This is very well articulated by the notion of "colonial feminism," as Leila Ahmed called it,[331] where people shed crocodile tears on behalf of women's oppression abroad while refraining from addressing sexism in their own land. In the French colonization of Algeria, the subject of Muslim oppression of women was used to rationalize the colonial mission, typical of the impulse—or rhetoric—of *mission civilizatrice*. And even George W. Bush and his wife, Laura—neither of whom are known for their feminist advocacy—exploited the plight of Muslim women in Afghanistan in order to pump up the United States to invade and occupy the country. Yet both fell silent about the plight of Afghanistan's women once the country was conquered by U.S. troops.

And the reason why Saudi Arabia and its women attract so much attention in the Western press and popular culture—but not among Western governments, which have covered up Saudi human rights violations for decades—is because Saudi Arabia, like the Taliban of recent years, represents Islam's extreme. As a British colonial ruler once observed: reformed Islam is no longer Islam. And mainstream Islam, as far as many people and organizations in the West are concerned, is not Islam either. Saudi Arabia serves as a useful reminder of how oppressed women are "over there," to perhaps remind women in the West of how "lucky we are here." Such sentiments were heard loudly in 2001 as the United States justified its war against Afghanistan.

In the Arab world, Saudi Arabia also receives attention; this is partly because Saudi propaganda campaigns are always lavish in attempts to try to soften the negative coverage of Saudi policies and practices and partly because Saudi Islam truly *is* extreme and most Muslims cannot identify with it— even those among the Muslim fundamentalists who decry the hypocrisy of the Saudi royal family.

THE SAUDI VERSION OF MALE SUPREMACY

Even by the standards of conservative Muslim scholars in the Middle East, Saudi Arabia's Islamic patriarchy is harsh and extreme and must be understood in the context of Wahhabiyyah. The best representative of the Wahhabi doctrine and its impact on women is the influential Mufti Shaykh `Abdul-`Aziz Bin Baz. Bin Baz was the epitome of obscurantist thought—somebody who, as mentioned earlier, rejected that a man had set foot on the moon and long insisted that the earth was flat.[332] On the subject of women, Bin Baz was, not unlike other theologians of Wahhabiyyah, harsh and inflexible. In their minds—not unlike the thinking in some branches of Orthodox Judaism—any part of a woman, including for some her voice, is pudendum (`awrah`), which should never be exposed except to a very small number of family members. Bin Baz prohibited arts and photography, and the theologians of Wahhabiyyah did not want radio and TV in the kingdom but later changed their minds once they became convinced that they could be used for purposes of religious indoctrination, which explains the unpopularity of Saudi TV, with its heavy dosage of Islamic "evangelism." Women are still prohibited from driving cars lest they find themselves freely roaming public space in the company of "strange" men.[333] On this subject, Bin Baz was quite unequivocal:

> This hadith points out what we have been saying about the dangers of mixing boys and girls at all levels of instruction. The evidence for that from the Quran, sunnah and the experience of the ummah today are many but I do not wish to mention them all here in order to be brief. The knowledge of our government, may Allah give them understanding, as well as the Minister of Education and the President of the Directory for Girls Education is sufficient for us to go into this matter here. I ask Allah to grant us all what is good for this ummah. And to make us and our male and female youth good. And to give them happiness in both this life and the Hereafter. He is the Hearer, Responder. And peace and blessings be upon our Prophet Muhammad and his family and Companion.[334]

Saudi Arabia's political formula allows the religious establishment to have the final say on the subject of gender and sexuality. And when the government tried in 2001 to introduce identity cards for women to facilitate their further incorporation into the workplace, a furor ensued when the religious establishment decreed that it was impermissible to have women's images on identity cards.[335] The royal family had to postpone the procedure until further notice. And while many Muslim countries have incorporated Western laws into their code and have allowed for some reforms in the application of laws, Saudi Arabia remains quite inhospitable to the notion of gender-related legal reforms, out of fear of instigating a rift between the royal family and the religious core. And the nature of the marriage between the two sides is such that the royal family is allowed to rule, while the religious establishment exercises a monopoly over issues of religion and education.

EDUCATION

It must not be assumed that women in Saudi Arabia suffer the same plight as did the women under the Taliban regime in Afghanistan. Gradually but steadily, women in Saudi Arabia have increasingly been given access to various educational levels and tiers, although the fields of Islamic theology and jurisprudence elude them because the clerics insist that they are to be kept out of those fields. While there have been important strides in combating illiteracy among women, there is still a gap in literacy between men and women. According to 2003 estimates by the CIA, 78.8 percent of the overall population is literate; 84.7 percent of men are literate, while only 70.8 percent of women are literate.[336] Education is a staple of Islamic teachings; a famous hadith states that people should "seek knowledge even if you have to go all the way to China." Women's education was known in early Islam, and `A'ishah was quite learned, although she could not write. During his time, the Prophet Muhammad encouraged women to learn about religion, and he made available a special gate at his house for women who wanted to learn about Islam.[337] The struggle for learning in Saudi Arabia was one to be fought by men and women alike: one has to remember that higher education for men was not available until 1957. And the clerics were adamantly opposed to the education of women for decades after the founding of the kingdom. They argued that education would corrupt morals and bring about a breakdown of the family.[338] It was King Faysal and his wife who championed the cause of women's education and who pushed the clerics to change their minds. The first official primary school for girls was founded in Riyadh in 1960.[339] And after King Faysal's assumption to the throne in 1964, he presented a series of what was then considered reforms, many of which were rejected by the clerical establishment. But the compromise that Faysal reached with the clerics stipulated that the affairs of women's education would be in the hands of a committee staffed by the senior clerics and their representatives. The percentage of female students kept steadily increasing until it exceeded that of men in some areas. In 1988–90, for example, "69,054 female students graduated from secondary schools compared with 65,086 males."[340]

Table 6.1

WOMEN AND EDUCATION IN SAUDI ARABIA[341]

Educational Level	1970	1975	1980	1983	1995
Elementary	31%	36%	39%	41%	48%
Secondary	20%	33%	38%	39%	46%
College	8%	20%	28%	32%	46%

As can be seen, progress is being made in the field of education, although issues of sexism still mar the process of women's education in the kingdom. Men are more likely to receive state support to study abroad than women, although family, tribe, and tradition may also serve as strong barriers to women's quest for foreign education. Furthermore, the rising unemployment in the kingdom and the decline of oil wealth is adding pressures to the social system and may lead to a backlash against women's education and labor.

But women's education in Saudi Arabia must be understood within the context of the curriculum being taught, and this is still completely controlled by the fundamentalist Wahhabi clerical establishment. And there is evidence that popular support for the education of women is widespread in Saudi Arabia and elsewhere in the kingdom. In one comprehensive survey, some 90 percent of Saudi women surveyed maintained that education is "obligatory because it is so urged by religion."[342] The clerical establishment injects a heavy dosage of religious indoctrination into the curricula and only allows for its conservative and consistently sexist interpretations of religious texts. It is also unclear whether the increasing education of women will increase the pressure on the state to provide jobs for the new graduates. Moreover, as the government strictly enforces segregation in education, it seems safe to assume that more resources go to men's schools than to women's. One might also question the extent to which scientific fields get support in women's schools and colleges, in comparison to those of men.

Education for women underwent a change after the scandal in 2002 when trapped schoolgirls died in a fire because the moral police outside would not let them exit their burning school without wearing the proper Saudi-imposed religious attire. This resulted in a public outcry and led the government to place women's education under the Ministry of Education and not under the domain of the clerical establishment.

FAMILY AND SEXUALITY

It is often mistakenly assumed that the lives of Middle Eastern women are shaped *solely* by Islam and by its restrictive Shari`ah. In reality, no society is exclusively shaped by religion, nor is there such a thing as uniform religion. Islam, like other religions, morphs with the culture and traditions in the regions to which it spreads. Thus, Islam in Morocco is different from Islam in Indonesia, as Clifford Geertz has pointed out in his famous book *Islam Observed*.[343] The historic and cultural setting of Saudi Arabia has its own peculiarities; the birthplace of the Prophet Muhammad and the location of the two holy sites in the kingdom infuse a palpable religious (and clerical) intensity to the local culture. The political arrangement between the House of Saud and the Wahhabi clerics also reinforces the role of religion in society and upholds the exclusive monopoly of the Shari`ah in all matters of personal status laws.

Tradition weighs heavily on the ways in which Shari`ah is interpreted and applied in the kingdom. The clerical establishment often invokes tradition in order to press society and the government to adhere to Wahhabi legal and theological interpretations. At least some women in Saudi Arabia seem to be aware of the ways in which "traditions" have been used to justify and perpetuate male supremacy in the kingdom, as seen in Table 6.2 below.

It has to be pointed out that the very question about tradition is a loaded one; the clerical establishments and many Middle East governments have succeeded in preaching that tradition and religion are one and the same thing. So those women who express a willingness to challenge traditions are also challenging religion, regardless of whether they intend to or not.

Table 6.2[344]

PERCENTAGE OF WOMEN WHO
THINK THAT TRADITIONS OBSTRUCT
WOMEN'S PROGRESS

Country	Percentage (%)
Kuwait	34.9
Qatar	43.3
Bahrain	44.3
UAE	5.0
Saudi Arabia	50.0

There is in Saudi Arabia the notion of the guardianship, which is rooted to certain phrases in the Qur'an. These phrases stipulate that women are legally incomplete or inferior entities and that a male (he could be a father, husband, brother, uncle, or any other male relative) is legally in charge of the woman "under him." So a woman in Saudi Arabia has to obtain written permission from the male guardian to be allowed outside of the country and has to be accompanied by a legal relative even when venturing into a public space inside the kingdom. Other Arab countries also have this principle, although it is not strictly enforced in all of them.

To this day there remains an emphasis on the traditional marriage and family institution, which often implies the perpetuation of patriarchal structure through the family. As in other Muslim Arab countries, polygamy is permitted in Saudi Arabia, although the number of polygamous marriages in the kingdom, as elsewhere in the region, constitutes a small percentage of all marriages. Only wealthy members of the royal family and their business partners can afford to indulge in this traditional "luxury." Statistics about this practice and about attitudes toward it are lacking.

Traditional arranged marriages still exist in Saudi Arabia and elsewhere in the region, although there is little specific data in this regard. Traditional marriages entail an agreement between parents—often for business or political purposes—to marry off their daughters and sons, often with little consultation with them. Younger urban members of society are more likely to insist on their right to choose their own partners in marriage. In fact, in a survey of Gulf Arab women, Saudi women were the most insistent on selecting their own husbands by themselves.

Table 6.3

PERCENTAGE OF GULF ARAB WOMEN WHO PREFER TO
SELECT THEIR OWN HUSBAND, 1981–82[345]

Country	Percentage (%)
Bahrain	77.8
Kuwait	84.0
Qatar	90.3
UAE	87.5
Saudi Arabia	90.0

It is also noteworthy that according to the same study, a large majority of women in Arab Gulf countries also favor meeting their future husband before marriage, as illustrated in Table 6.4 below.

This should put to rest the stereotypical Western view of

Middle Eastern women relishing their own inferior status, and it should also challenge the Islamic fundamentalist

Table 6.4

PERCENTAGE OF WOMEN WHO PREFER TO MEET THEIR FUTURE HUSBAND BEFORE MARRIAGE[346]

Country	Percentage (%)
Kuwait	68.2
Qatar	82.3
Bahrain	66.7
UAE	87.5
Saudi Arabia	70.0

assumption regarding women's willingness to embrace traditions. The percentages derived from the study indicate a measure of sociopolitical nonconformity that may eventually add stress to the political system and in the long run bring about important changes. Crown Prince `Abdullah has recently made statements in which he paid lip service to the vague cause of addressing the plight of women in Saudi Arabia. We cannot view those recent statements by the crown prince of Saudi Arabia and his decision to consult with women delegations—an unprecedented political gesture—without taking into consideration the ways in which women in Saudi Arabia have expressed, by whatever means available, their views and opinions. And the crown prince has failed in making any substantial changes in the status of women anyway.

Segregation is another staple of Saudi society. Of course, segregation in Saudi Arabia is legally enforced, and the power

of the state, through the fearsome "morality police"—
mutawwa`ah—is employed to impose a harsh set of rules and
regulations pertaining to social habits and dress. To be sure,
those rules apply to both men and women, but they are more
stringent on women than on men. Segregation in other soci-
eties exists whenever males gather together and feel that there
are certain things that should not be shared with women; men
who go to strip joints are practicing a form of segregation too.
Segregation in Saudi Arabia is more extreme, of course, and
leaves women with a great disadvantage, because through segregation the clerical establishment and the royal family have
kept women out of major decision-making bodies that often
rule on issues dealing with women themselves. Also, a man has
a greater ability to violate rules of segregation because the
penalties of violation for women are always more harsh and
deal with the issues of honor and chastity. It is in this context
that the Saudi government is still very keen on enforcing the
ban on female driving.

EMPLOYMENT AND ECONOMICS

The Saudi government has been allowing more women in
the workforce. The ability of the clerical establishment to
confine women to their houses has suffered with the
increasing educational attainments by women. In addition
to that, the kingdom has been trying to reduce the size of the
foreign workforce, which according to figures from the Saudi
Ministry of Planning stood at 3.56 million in 1989.[347] The
size of the foreign workforce in the kingdom became an
issue both for political and economic reasons. Politically,
the government became sensitive to the criticism of allow-

ing such a large number of foreigners, many of whom are not even Muslims. This is always a sensitive issue to the royal family and was especially so when it came under attack by dissidents enraged over the presence of U.S. troops in the kingdom. In addition, the presence of foreign workers has become an issue of economic and political stress since at least the 1990s, with the advent of the economic downturn and the rising unemployment in the kingdom. For the benefit of economic security, many Saudis are now even willing to accept what used to be considered "dirty jobs."

And the percentage of women in the workforce seems to be on the increase. By 1976, for example, women constituted some 21 percent of Kuwait's labor force.[348] But the figures from Saudi Arabia are much lower. The 1989–90 Five Year Development Plan aimed at increasing the female participation rate in the civilian economic sector to 6 percent by 1994–95.[349] More and more women are pursuing careers, perhaps because their ability to rely on men in the family has been diminished as the kingdom's economic problems increase. While *The Economist* estimates the number of working women to be around a quarter of a million, it has reported increasing desires by women to enter into the business sector. In two cities alone, Riyadh and Jeddah, six thousand business licenses were issued to women in 1998.[350] This is while women face tremendous obstacles in the workplace: they cannot deal directly with men; they have to have a male "guardian" sponsor; and they, of course, cannot drive and have to depend on a man for their transportation.

There is also evidence of increasing support by women for work, as seen in Table 6.5.

It should also be pointed out that certain factors might

inhibit the willingness of women to admit support for more women in the labor force. Such a view may indicate a lower class status; for example, wealthy women may associate work-

Table 6.5

PERCENTAGE OF WOMEN WHO SUPPORT
WOMEN IN THE LABOR FORCE[351]

Country	Percentage (%)
Kuwait	61.3
Qatar	74.2
Bahrain	55.6
UAE	37.5
Saudi Arabia	40.0

ing women with poverty and need. And some high-ranking members of the government are now quite open about their support for women's work. The second deputy commander of the National Guard, for example, asserted that there is "nothing in Islam that forbids a woman from working; in fact, the contrary is true. To arbitrarily prevent a woman from working is against Islam."[352]

Not much data exists about women and work in Saudi Arabia, although Abdella Doumato has shed some light on the subject. She reports that the public sector remains the largest employer of women (and men, of course) and that "the vast majority who work are in the sex-segregated education system where their numbers are growing as Saudis replace foreign nationals."[353]

HEALTH

We do not have much information on the health conditions of women in Saudi Arabia. Investigation of such matters offends the intention of the clerics to keep such information private. The kingdom has had first-rate medical care, which is provided free to all citizens. We do not know what particular diseases afflict women, although reports of health problems and obesity due to the change of diet after the introduction of fast food have been published. AIDS cases are shrouded in secrecy, although they seem to have struck less than 0.01 percent of the population.

VEILING

Veiling has become a symbol for the oppression of women in the Muslim world. Recent events in Afghanistan have focused too much attention on the veil (in its various forms), often implying that discarding the veil is the true measure of women's liberation and gender equality. Such a view, of course, is too superficial to be taken seriously. Feminism should aim at rendering female dress irrelevant from our judgment of women, and some Western feminists, like the Feminist Majority, place so much emphasis on veiling, as if dress is useful to summarize the life and conditions of women. Just as the dress of women in the West is not indicative of whether they are oppressed or not, the existence of the veil itself should not necessarily imply conditions of oppression. This is not to say that veiling is not sexist: it is when imposed. The veil is also sexist because it implies a sexual objectification of women: that they have to be covered to reduce the chances of male sexual arousal. Similarly, Western media ubiquitously advertise dress as a method to increase sexiness, which means that in both systems male arousal—sex and sexism—determine the dress system. Of course, in the West the state does not enforce a dress code, but social enforcement may be as strong.

While in Saudi Arabia the dress code is imposed by the state and women do not have the option to reject it, evidence from other Arab and Muslim countries indicates that veiling may occur for a variety of reasons: (1) to reduce the threat of verbal and physical sexual harassment on the streets—of course, women should be immune from that regardless of how they dress; (2) as enforcement of a belief that religiosity requires veiling; (3) because of pressures from members of the family; (4) as a way of following traditions or laws in a particular place; or (5) to avoid a fashion competition with wealthier women in the school or workplace. Poorer women find it easier to don the long loose cover; it's a way of opting out of expensive Western-style clothing.

POLITICS AND LAW

It is easy to dismiss the subject of civil liberties from this section. After all, neither men nor women have political rights in Saudi Arabia. But the climate of oppression affects everybody concerned in the kingdom, and human rights organizations have documented cases of arbitrary arrests, regular executions, and torture.[354] The government's institutionalized prejudice and sexism are often embedded in the laws. These laws explicitly discriminate "against women in almost all aspects of life: decision making, employment, education and family relationships."[355] And the Basic Law that introduced the consultative council in 1993 ignores the presence of women in the population, even though women have expressed their defiance against the state on a number of occasions. Ironically, outside of the kingdom, Saudi women can pursue more opportunities commensurate with their talents and skills. In October 2000, UN Secretary-General Kofi Annan appointed Thuraya Ahmad Obeid as an executive director for the United Nations Population Fund. Certainly, Ms. Obeid would have been unable to work as a staff member of such an important organization inside the kingdom.

There is evidence that Saudi women are becoming more vocal in demanding their rights. In the proliferating Arab satellite media, one often hears Saudi women callers arguing passionately over political issues. For example, one survey indicates that Saudi women are quite opposed to minority rule, as illustrated in Table 6.6.

Table 6.6

PERCENTAGE OF WOMEN WHO
OPPOSE MINORITY RULE[356]

Country	Percentage (%)
Bahrain	55.6
Kuwait	49.8
Qatar	59.7
UAE	50.0
Saudi Arabia	70.0

The same survey also indicates that some 60 percent of Saudi women reject the notion that politics should be the exclusive concern of men and that men should be in charge of political affairs.[357] Such figures and surveys, often published and conducted in Arabic, are missing from the literature on the subject, thereby perpetuating the stereotype of Saudi women passively and silently endorsing their own exclusion. In 2003, the Saudi government began to consider the idea that women can attend—merely attend—the sessions of the Shura Council.

OUTLOOK FOR THE TWENTY-FIRST CENTURY

It is unlikely that democratic change will come to the kingdom soon; it is also unlikely that the plight of Saudi women will mobilize U.S. policy makers who suddenly expressed concern for the plight of Afghani women, but not for the plight of Iraqi women, who most likely will see their plight regress with the rise of Islamic fundamentalism and patriarchal cultural values as a result of the U.S. invasion and occupation. In early 2004, women were demonstrating in Baghdad against a new rule issued by the U.S.-formed so-called Iraqi Governing Council, which replaced the old secular family code with a new one that imposes the sexist personal status laws of the various sects.[358] In fact, such blatant exploitation of the subject of Muslim women can only increase the suspicions among many in the region toward Western feminism, and eventually help in discrediting local feminists who are linked in the minds of many to the colonial and domineering interests of Western powers. The struggle for gender liberty and equality is, of course, as alive in Saudi Arabia as it is elsewhere. But the presence of oil, and Western support for the oppressive Saudi government, only make the struggle more difficult. Women are doubly oppressed in Saudi Arabia because, as the next chapter shows, on one level, *everyone* there is oppressed.

In 2004 the Saudi government was debating some very minor aspects of women's rights, for example, whether some women should be allowed to attend the meetings of the Shura Council. But the fundamental sexism of the Saudi system remains unchanged, and the royal family continues to express its commitment to "traditions."

SEVEN

Opposition and Inhumane (Lack of) Rights

DISSENT

The Saudi power balance faced problems from the very moment the state was created, and its political system has failed to accommodate the demands to change and evolve. The first opposition to the Saudi state was tribal, and the Saud tribe committed their first atrocities, massacres, and human rights violations, crushing their opponents, long before they succeeded in forming a state and establishing their royalty. No distinction was made between civilians and combatants during the Wahhabi-Saudi wars of conquest on the Arabian peninsula. Tribes and families that opposed the Saud family were evicted or killed.

The new kingdom's first dissident groups were the conquered tribes—the persecuted Shi`ites and the Ikhwan—who resented the domination of the Saudi family and the moral deviations that were perceived in them. The first signs of secular opposition in Saudi Arabia were detected in the 1950s, during the Arab nationalist stirrings. ARAMCO workers went on strike in 1953 and 1956; demands ranged from improvement of workers' conditions to nationalization of oil resources.[359] For the Arab nationalists in Saudi Arabia, communists, Nasserists, Ba`thists, and others, the goal was a republican government that would sever Saudi ties with the West and strive toward Arab unity. Ending the rule of the royal family was a goal shared by Nasser and his Ba`thist rivals. Saudi response to dissent has always been brutally swift and ruthless. Trials are quick, and vague accusations are sufficient to indict and execute.

From the 1950s until the collapse of the Soviet Union, communist organizations operated in small secret cells within the kingdom. The 1953 labor strike sparked communist organization and produced the communist-leaning Reform Front, which later changed its name to National Liberation Front, and then reemerged as the Communist Party in 1975.[360] Communist opposition literature, especially of the Saudi Communist Party, was filled with detailed critiques of the Saudi economy, tributes to the then motherland of communism, critiques of women's oppression in the kingdom, and attacks on the Western orientation of the corrupt royal family.[361] The Saudi communists organized the workers in illegal unions,[362] although there are no trade union rights in Saudi Arabia.[363] And the leftist (and Arab nationalist) opposition often overlapped with the Shi`ite cleavage in the kingdom. Shi`ite resentment against the oppression of the community expressed itself in attraction to all ideologies of opposition. Thus, Shi`ites constituted the bulk of the members of the Saudi Communist Party, the (Marxist-Leninist) Socialist Arab Action Party, and the Ba`th Party.[364] There are no indications that communist organizations have been active in Saudi Arabia in recent years, although Saudi communists remain active as individuals.

Another left-leaning nationalist organization was the Union of the People of Arabia, which was founded in 1958 and headed by Nasir As-Sa`id.[365] It was active often outside of Saudi Arabia, given the severity of repression. As-Sa`id, as

was mentioned earlier, was reportedly kidnapped and killed by
Saudi intelligence in 1979. But the heyday of nationalist and
leftist dissidence seems to have been in the 1960s, when
Nasser energized the anti-Saudi camp inside and outside Saudi
Arabia. The liberal princes were also part of the dissent movement in the 1960s, and liberal Prince Talal was even linked to
the 1969 military coup attempt.

The religious opposition movement has had an easier time
in Saudi Arabia. Its symbols and motifs are easier to transmit
and explain. They organize within mosques and religious
schools without having to worry about their meeting places
being busted. They can speak the language of official
Wahhabiyyah Islam even if they disagree with the government.
Of course, the range of the religious-oriented dissent is quite
wide: it spans from armed extremes like Bin Ladin to sincere
religious reformers who resent the corruption and hypocrisy of
the House of Saud. Most of this type of movement occurs underground because there were no earlier indications of the dissent
of Juhayman Al-`Utaybi before he stormed into the Grand
Mosque in 1979. Or, it is fair to say that while the government
knew of `Utaybi's arguments (even if he concealed his revolu-
tionary and messianic beliefs), it ignored him. Up until 1979
the government was more concerned about dissent in the armed
forces (especially after the 1969 coup attempt) and leftist and
Arab nationalist dissent.

Religious dissent is largely co-opted by the government by
virtue of its lavish spending on religious schools and propaganda. Religious opposition to the royals focuses on the domestic situation, and their keen interest in the application of
Wahhabi dogma, even if this entails, for example, an increased
persecution of Shi`ites. This was something that Juhayman Al-
`Utaybi specifically mentioned in his writings, before leading

the 1979 rebellion in Mecca. The Iranian revolution seems to have influenced both Saudi Sunnis and Shi`ites. The Shi`ites felt energized with the success of a Shi`ite model of government, which brought a heightened sense of self-confidence and self-esteem to the community. It also affected Shi`ite links to the outside world with Khomeini's call for the export of revolution. For the Sunnis, it also led to an increase in their religious mobilization, and the model, while Shi`ite, served the cause of those who were calling for application of Shari`ah (Islamic laws).

U.S. foreign policy has had a potent impact on Saudi Arabia. The Gulf War of 1991 produced an ideological polarization in the kingdom: it split the core opposition into liberal and fundamentalist fronts. The latter category has shades and streaks within its ranks, ranging from those who agree with Al-Qa'idah to those who want an increased role of religion in society, without using violence. The liberal front was energized in the first Gulf War when it presented the king with a list of demands, seeking, for the most part, to end corruption. The liberals' approach has been to avoid criticizing foreign policy in order to increase the credibility of their domestic agenda. Similarly, the fundamentalists tend to focus on domestic issues too. But lately, both fronts have turned their opposition toward foreign policy as well.

Another by-product of the first U.S. Gulf War was the creation of the Committee for the Defense of Legitimate Rights in Saudi Arabia (CDLR) in 1993.[366] The founders included "two university professors, a retired judge and religious scholars."[367] Initially, the committee stressed the need for application of Shari`ah and spoke in general virtuous terms, but later became more radical. Its two main leaders are Muhammad Al-Mas`ari and Sa`d Al-Faqih. Muhammad Al-Mas`ari is a

German-educated physicist and son of a retired judge who lived in the United States for a while. He has been very adept at utilizing the modern media and technology to spread his group's message but has been hampered by lack of "tribal qualification"[368] and charges of Western links that stem from his European education and his stay in the United States during his youth. Al-Faqih is a medical doctor who was impressed with the Iranian revolution and grew unhappy with what he saw in Saudi society.[369] Those two and other supporters quickly made a name for their group, and the CDLR was just as quickly banned in Saudi Arabia.[370] The royal family immediately got the highest religious authorities in the kingdom to issue a condemnation of the group. After arrests and harassment, the group relocated to London in 1994, where it distinguished itself with great PR work for its cause.

CDLR's message has been inconsistent and hypocritical; for Arabic audiences it speaks of Shari`ah and Islamic laws and mores, and for the Western audiences it speaks strictly in terms of human rights and democracy. In fact, its use of the word "legitimate" in its name may not connote what the word signifies in English: it is a loose translation of the word that carries the meaning of Shari`ah. The first statement of the group clearly speaks of people's rights, as they are enshrined not in the Universal Declaration of Human Rights but in the group's interpretation of Islamic laws. It also believes that human rights violation in Saudi Arabia has harmed "the image of Islam in the minds of many people."[371] Its members lament the lack of legal vehicles for political expression, and the lack of rights and condemn the recent oppression and persecution in the kingdom. They also made clear that they are concerned only about conditions in Saudi Arabia, but since their relocation to London they have added the entire Arabian peninsula to its concerns.[372] Al-Mas`ari fine-tuned his skill in getting messages out through Western media (as he is ignored by the largely Saudi-funded Arab media), and his group maintains an extremely well developed Web site, which contains a full body of political literature produced or endorsed by the group.[373]

Al-Mas`ari develops his views in his major work, *Al-Adillah Al-Qat`iyyah `Ala `Adam Shar`iyyat Ad-Dawla-s-Sa`udiyyah* (*The Decisive Proofs on the Illegality of the Saudi State*).[374] The book is a classic fundamentalist critique of the Saudi kingdom, and it attacks the Saudi's "lax" application of Islamic law. Laughingly, Al-Mas`ari even accuses the royal family of spreading "secular" messages in its media and rejects as usury any form of interest-charging banking. Al-Mas`ari makes many references to "infidels," referring not only to non-Muslims but also to the United Nations and its organizations. He adheres to a very conservative and strict branch of Islamic jurisprudence and uses that standard to attack the corruption of the House of Saud. This language of strict Islamic fundamentalism Al-Mas`ari saves for his Arabic writings, just as he sticks to the language of human rights when speaking to Western media.

The group suffered a setback in 1996 when Al-Mas`ari allegedly expelled Al-Faqih for going soft on the royal family and having secret contacts with Crown Prince `Abdullah. The differences were also over the scope of the group's work: with Al-Mas`ari wanting to branch out to other Muslim organizations and areas and Al-Faqih wanting to confine the work to Saudi Arabia.[375] Al-Faqih established his own group, the Movement for Islamic Reform (MIRA), in 1996. Apparently, the split was detrimental to the work of the group, but the Movement, like the CDLR, continued to operate a very rich and accessible Web site that posts its political literature.[376]

The site distributes an Islamic critique of the conditions inside the kingdom and explicitly identifies media technology as their method of oppositional struggle, eschewing any other political or military methods. The group's attitude toward Shi`ites is unfavorable, although it does not call for the declaration of their infidelity.[377] The movement, however, must have some roots inside the kingdom as it puts out information about very specific events and episodes, and details the human rights violations in the country. MIRA is even keen on reporting every incidence of adultery, attempted adultery, homosexuality, attempted homosexuality, kidnappings, possession of pornographic materials, abortions, rape, prostitution, harassment, transsexuality, and "morally illegal" entries into residences as solid proof of the inability of the government to enforce "the moral standards."[378] The movement also finds it important to state that there were some 8,378 cases of reported alcohol consumption in one year A.H. 1423 (2002).[379] It is not easy, however, to evaluate the extent to which people inside the country support either the CDLR or the Movement for Islamic Reform. Al-Faqih calls for "the restructuring" of the Saudi regime but not for its abolishment.[380] Others state that Al-Faqih is very critical of the country's subservient clerics and of Ibn Baz in particular,[381] but the official mouthpiece carried a laudatory obituary of Ibn Baz and praised him for spreading the Islamic fundamentalist principles (*salafiyyah*, return to the path of the virtuous ancestors, a key doctrine closely associated with Wahhabiyyah dogma).[382]

In 2003 Al-Faqih's organization proved to have active members inside the kingdom. Through a radio station in Lebanon, he beamed messages of opposition and defiance into the kingdom and succeeded a few times in calling on people to demonstrate against the government. All those who responded to his calls were summarily arrested by the police.

The Shi`ite opposition in Saudi Arabia ebbs and flows; it was energized after the Islamic revolution in Iran and was later—especially a segment of the Shi`ite opposition—co-opted and bought by the Saudi government in the wake of the Gulf War of 1991, and there is evidence that the movement has been recently becoming more vocal in expressing its demands for more political participation and minority rights and religious celebrations. The movement's expressions of their goals seem to have changed around the late 1980s, when, under the leadership of Shaykh Hasan As-Saffar, they began to move away from the pro-Iranian revolutionary rhetoric toward more reformist polemics.[383] As-Saffar has written extensively (although he is published outside the kingdom), and his treatise on political pluralism signals the change from radicalism toward an accommodation of liberal democratic thought.[384] The mouthpiece of the Shi`ite liberal group, *Al-Jazirah Al-`Arabiyyah*, reflected the trend of accommodation and reform, and called for negotiations and dialogue with the Saudi government.[385] The magazines mostly dealt with issues of corruption and human rights violation and gradually became less vocal against the Saudi royal family.[386] In the summer of 1994 the offices of the group in London and the United States were closed, and the leaders and members moved back to Saudi Arabia. When then asked by the author whether it was true that they had been co-opted and bought off by the Saudi royal family, the Washington, D.C., members laughed and confirmed that indeed they had made up with the king. Later on, as a gesture toward the group, Ibn Baz met with Shaykh As-Saffar.[387] The Shi`ite opposition has become more vocal in the last few years, and the rise of Hezbollah as a popular pan-Arab party has increased the esteem of Shi`ites in the Arab world. The rise of Shi`ite power in Iraq will also reflect favorably on the political significance of the Shi`ites of Saudi Arabia, who regularly contact Al-Jazeera TV and other Arab satellite channels to air their grievances and complain about the discrimination they face.

The Al-Qa`idah phenomenon is more difficult to study and assess, and I have dealt with it elsewhere.[388] As the group is banned and its members pursued by Saudi security services, one cannot measure the extent to which they have succeeded in extending their influence in the country. The fact that the Saudi government has fired hundreds of preachers and religious teachers since September 11 indicates that there is a current of support for Bin Ladin's message among the Sunni religious ranks. That even the clerical descendant of Muhammad Ibn `Abdul-Wahab has been railing against the extremists and the "deviationists" reflects a level of worry and fear on the part of the government and its allies.[389] Al-Qa`idah and Bin Ladin expose the weak position of the clerics, and their subservience to the House of Saud. The clerics cannot but feel insecure when they hear Bin Ladin competing with them in religious propaganda and advocacy. But it is not clear how the Saudi battle against Al-Qa`idah is advancing; the government is never candid in its statements that seem only to spread news that favors the stance of the royal family no matter what exists in reality. And Prince Sultan's claim that "80 percent of the terrorists" have been eliminated cannot be substantiated given the long record of lies and fabrications by the House of Saud.

HUMAN RIGHTS

The abysmal human rights conditions inside the kingdom have remained stagnant and constant for years, if not for decades.

This is how the March 2003 U.S. Department of State's *Country Reports on Human Rights Practices* describes the situation in Saudi Arabia:

> The Government's human rights record remained poor; although there were some improvements in a few areas, serious problems remained. Citizens did not have the right or the legal means to change their government. Security forces continued to abuse detainees and prisoners, arbitrarily arrest and detain persons, and hold them in incommunicado detention. Security forces committed torture.... Prolonged detention without charge was a problem. Security forces committed such abuses, in contradiction to the law, but with the acquiescence of the Government. The Mutawwa'in continued to intimidate, abuse, and detain citizens and foreigners. Most trials were closed, and defendants usually appeared before judges without legal counsel. The Government infringed on citizens' privacy rights. The Government prohibited or restricted freedom of speech, the press, assembly, association, religion, and movement. However, during the year, the Government continued to tolerate a wider range of debate and criticism in the press concerning domestic issues. Discrimination and violence against women, discrimination against ethnic and religious minorities, and strict limitations on worker rights continued.[390]

With this as the U.S. government's official view, one wonders why George W. Bush insisted in a recent phone conversation with Crown Prince `Abdullah that the relationship between the two countries is one of "eternal friendship." One also notices that despite the harsh reality of human rights abuse in Saudi Arabia, the Department of State's report makes an effort to shield the Saudi government and to dilute the severity of oppression. For example, while the report speaks about "allegation of torture" in Saudi Arabia, the same report is far less restrained in its language when dealing with Libya. The report states: "Security personnel routinely torture prisoners" and "traditional attitudes and practices prevailed, and discrimination against women persisted."[391] One notices that the U.S. government is far more open in highlighting human rights abuses in the dictatorial government of Libya than in Saudi Arabia, which has a worse human rights record than most countries in the world. On women's issues, one notices that the government is even critical of "traditional attitudes" against women in Libya, which has a far better record on women's rights than Saudi Arabia, but does not refer to the institutional sexism and misogyny in Saudi Arabia, which is sanctioned and endorsed by the government.

One can refer to human rights reports on Saudi Arabia with little concern for the year of the release of the report. For example, the Minnesota Lawyers International Human Rights Committee's 1992 report on Saudi Arabia is far more objective and accurate than the U.S. Department of State's report:

> Saudi Arabia maintains a deplorable human rights situation for its citizens and foreign residents. Saudi Arabia remains an absolute monarchy with no penal code, no political parties, no freedom of religion, no trade unions, and no free press. Political and cultural dissent is harshly repressed. Even the thousands of refugees who fled from neighboring Iraq during the

Gulf crisis continue to be detained in desert camps surrounded by barbed-wire.[392]

Saudi Arabia has also set itself apart from other nations by (a) invoking Islam—that is, its strict interpretation of its Wahhabi version of Islam—as its overall jurisprudential guide, and (b) refusing to sign or adopt almost all important international human rights treaties and conventions.[393] Amnesty International has repeatedly called upon the international community to focus attention on Saudi Arabia. It states: "The scale and gravity of human rights violations in Saudi Arabia is untenable by any legal or moral standard." And it chides the international community for failing to "hold Saudi Arabia to account for its persistent violations of human rights."[394]

The human rights violations in the kingdom have been "exacerbated by the government policy of 'combating terrorism' in the wake of the 11 September 2001 attacks in the United States. The violations were perpetuated by the strictly secretive criminal justice system and the prohibition of political parties, trade unions, and independent human rights organizations. Hundreds of suspected religious activists and critics of the state were arrested, and the legal status of most of those held from previous years remained shrouded in secrecy."[395]

Some laws in the kingdom do in fact incorporate non-Islamic Western laws despite the official claim to the contrary. For example, there is a category of crimes in Saudi Arabia that is defined as *hudud* (boundaries) crimes, and they include: "consumption of alcohol, theft, armed robbery, adultery, defamation, and apostasy from Islam."[396] These crimes have fixed punishments (and it is not true, as the Minnesota Lawyers International Human Rights Committee maintains, that they are all specified in the Qur'an or Sunnah).[397] Those convicted of such a category of crimes cannot be pardoned. This explains the strict regularity of capital punishment in Saudi Arabia, as illustrated in Tables 7.1 and 7.2.

Table 7.1

EXECUTIONS IN SAUDI ARABIA[398]

Year	Number of Executions
1980	63
1981	14
1982	16
1983	21
1984	23
1985	45
1986	24
1987	54
1988	26
1989	111
1990	15
1991	29
1992	66
1993	88
1994	53
1995	192
1996	69
1997	122
1998	29
1999	103

Table 7.2

EXECUTIONS FOR DRUG-RELATED
OFFENSES IN SAUDI ARABIA[399]

Year	Number of Executions
1990	9
1991	3
1992	13
1993	53
1994	22
1995	98
1996	8
1997	54
1998	0
1999	51

Executions are conducted usually on Fridays after the noon prayers, to "attract people in public squares where the execution order takes place."[400] Saudi Arabia retains one of the highest rates of execution in "both absolute numbers and per capita."[401] And instead of respecting UN GA Resolution 32/61 of December 1977 that called for progressive reduction in the categories of capital offenses, Saudi Arabia has in fact "expanded the scope of [the] death penalty to a wide range of offenses, including offenses without lethal consequences."[402] Amnesty International counted some 560 executions in Saudi Arabia between January 1990 and July 1997 (although it concedes that the true figure is probably much higher).[403] There is also a racist pattern in the executions: European whites are less likely to be affected, while the majority of victims are foreign workers from Asia and Africa.[404] Executions also affect political prisoners; in 1988 the Saudi government executed four citizens for "conspiring against their country."[405]

Another facet of human rights violations in Saudi Arabia stems from the weakness and lack of independence or credibility for the judicial system; the king is the ultimate arbitrator and judge. He alone can appoint and remove judges within the kingdom. There is also evidence of close coordination and cooperation between the judiciary and the police and intelligence services in the kingdom; their words always supersede the accounts and statements of the accused.[406]

Within the kingdom, institutional legal inequality blatantly favors royal over nonroyal, Sunni over Shi`ite, male over female, citizen over noncitizen, rich over poor, and loyal over dissident. The royal family is clearly above the law and is not subject to the inspection or searches that other Saudis are subjected to when they enter the kingdom.[407] One person reports how "his refusal to forgo a debt owed to him by a prince led to his imprisonment and torture."[408] And the lack of written and specific codes of law also increases the arbitrary powers of the government, and also of the judiciary, which is always subordinate to the power of the king.

Torture is commonplace in Saudi Arabia. In 1990 "hundreds of Yemenis [had] reportedly been ill-treated or tortured in makeshift detention centers in Saudi Arabia and thousands [had] been arbitrarily arrested for no apparent reason other than their nationality."[409] Torture can range from flogging (even of children) to lashes and bodily mutilation.[410] Of course, with torture comes coerced confessions; when suspects refuse to confess to crimes, they are "intimidated, harassed, and repeatedly tortured, and may be held without trial indefinitely until they confess."[411]

In sum, Saudi Arabia remains one of the worst violators of human rights worldwide and yet continues to enjoy "eternal friendship" from the United States and friendly relations with many countries in Europe. It seems to be immune from the criticisms that other gross violators of human rights receive. This is true not only of the United States and other Western countries but also of international organizations, including the UN and its secretary-general.

EIGHT

U.S.-Saudi Relations

The House of Saud did not seem to anticipate September 11 and its consequences. There is no evidence that the Saudi royals are tied to the attackers or that they were in any way behind the bombings. Some relatives and survivors of the victims will try to prove otherwise in U.S. courts, motivated no doubt by greed and desire for revenge. The Saudi government, however, can be expected to be protected by the White House and highly paid consultants, lobbyists, and lawyers. Yes, the highly influential Prince Turki Bin Faysal resigned—or was ousted—from his job as head of the Saudi foreign intelligence agency. Turki had been a close operator with both the U.S. government and the international Islamic fundamentalist network, which he himself—in close cooperation with the CIA—had helped create, finance, train, and arm in response to the Soviet invasion of Afghanistan. He had the full support of King Fahd to do what was necessary to defeat Soviet forces and please the United States. The election of Ronald Reagan also elevated U.S.-Saudi relations to a higher strategic level, and Reagan's presidency coincided with the rise of King Fahd and the Sudayri Seven— staunch supporters of U.S.-Saudi relations. But an account of the history of U.S.-Saudi relations begins long before the Reagan administration and long before 9-11.

Early Saudi-American contacts can be traced back to the late nineteenth century and to the efforts of American missionaries who traveled from Basrah, as a base, to parts of Arabia. But they were more present in Bahrain than in what is today Saudi Arabia because that part of the peninsula was less hospitable to foreign presence and was geographically far less accessible. Diplomatic contacts, however, between the United States and the Saudi family did not begin before World War II, and Ibn Saud was closely linked with his British benefactors. The discovery of oil in the kingdom and the signing of an agreement with a U.S. oil company in 1933 put Saudi Arabia under the U.S. microscope for the first time. The Lebanese-American writer and first Arabic hagiographer of Ibn Saud, Amin Rihani, lobbied the U.S. government and the secretary of state in 1931 to recognize Ibn Saud. It was interesting to find in an internal declassified U.S. document that the State Department demanded to know the manner in which justice was administered in the kingdom before officially recognizing the kingdom.[412] Negotiations began between U.S. representatives and the Egyptian Hafidh Wahbah, the diplomatic advisor to Ibn Saud; the United States officially recognized Saudi Arabia in 1931 and the two countries signed a friendship and trade treaty in 1933. The presence of the American oil companies increased the influence of the United States in Saudi affairs, which coincided with the waning of the British empire. American oil companies constituted from the very beginning a pro-Saudi lobbying interest in Washington and have continued to play that role over the decades.

The rise of American influence in Saudi affairs was reflected in 1943 when the United States—unimaginable today—extended foreign assistance to Ibn Saud, who had been relying on British payments. Before the discovery of oil, Saudi Arabia could depend only on dates and pilgrimage income for its revenue. By the end of World War II, the total of American aid to Saudi Arabia reached $33,008,507.[413]

Official U.S. representation in Saudi Arabia, at the level of chargé d'affaires, commenced in 1943. World War II led oil executives in Saudi Arabia to lobby for the establishment of an American air base in the eastern sector (where the oil fields are located), and negotiations over military cooperation and coordination began in earnest. This inevitably created friction between the United States and the UK,[414] but the United States was determined by then, after years of accepting British influence in Arabia, and aided by its victory in the war, to establish control over Saudi Arabia no matter what. That Ibn Saud had signed an arms agreement with Hitler and Mussolini[415] and that he had clearly flirted with Hitler (Crown Prince `Abdullah keeps in his displayed possession a dagger given to him as a gift by Hitler[416]) did not disturb the American government, and Ibn Saud managed to stay on good terms with the UK.

The Palestinian question, and American support for Zionism at the expense of Arab rights, did not bother Ibn Saud much. Like all the other loyal pro-British rulers, he gave emotional speeches while doing nothing to actually tip the balance in favor of the Palestinians. And just as most pro-British rulers tried to kill off Palestinian revolutionary spirit, Ibn Saud urged the Palestinians to halt their revolt when the 1936–39 rebellion began. He famously telegrammed the Palestinian leader the following message: "To our sons, the Arabs of Palestine.... We have been very hurt by the current situation in Palestine, and we, in agreement with Arab kings and [Jordanian] Prince `Abdullah, call upon you to resort to quiet, and to end the strike to save blood; relying on God and the good intentions of our friend the British government, and its declared desire to achieve justice. Trust that we shall keep trying to help you."[417] In 1943 he admitted to an American reporter that he had been largely silent about the Palestinian problem to avoid putting the Arabs "in a position that would embarrass [the UK and the United States]."[418] His help for the British—and indirectly for the Zionists—was not based on any love for Zionism or Jews. In fact, he harbored the same anti-Semitism that his sons inherited, and that is a mainstay of Saudi political literature and media. He once observed that Jews are "a race accursed by God, according to his Holy Book, and destined to final destruction and eternal damnation."[419] Declassified British documents contain a plethora of anti-Semitic outbursts by Ibn Saud, and King Faysal was willing to share his views about global Jewish conspiracies with everybody who stepped into his office, including Henry Kissinger.[420]

During this period Ibn Saud's son Prince Faysal visited Washington, D.C., to solidify U.S.-Saudi relations. The Palestinian question was not discussed, but bilateral ties were enhanced. By then the Saudi family knew that the future—and their regular subsidies—would lie with the Americans. To this day, the watershed moment in the history of U.S.-Saudi relations remains the meeting between FDR and Ibn Saud. It was the first time that Ibn Saud, sixty-nine at the time, had met a non-Muslim head of state. There were unlimited American accounts of the ninety-three sheep that Ibn Saud insisted on accompanying him on the U.S. ship that took him to meet the American president. As Ibn Saud finished watching a U.S. propaganda documentary (while his sons were watching nondocumentaries without their father's knowledge), he commented about movies: "I doubt whether my people should have moving pictures like this.... It would give them an appetite for entertainment which might distract them from their religious duties."[421] All of Ibn Saud's successors agreed with him, and movies have yet to be permitted in Saudi Arabia. As every American president had done, even before the founding of Israel, FDR took the opportunity to push the Zionist cause in the meeting. Ibn Saud could not understand why, in his mind, the president seemed intent on punishing the Palestinians for Hitler's crimes. The Saudi king had to remind the American president, who severely restricted Jewish immigration into the United States even while he was aware of the Holocaust, that Germans, not Palestinians, had committed the atrocities against Jews in Europe. After the meeting, an American official present reported that Ibn Saud stood and shook Roosevelt's hand and asked him to swear to "never support the Zionists in Palestine against the Arabs."[422] Roosevelt later told Congress, with more than a tinge of insincerity, that: "... from Ibn Saud, of Arabia, I learned more of the whole problem of the Moslems and more about the Jewish problem in 5 minutes than I could have learned by the exchange of a dozen letters."[423]

Ibn Saud took a liking to FDR, especially compared to Churchill, who offended several of his Wahhabi sensibilities in the course of one meal, and who, given his long track record in the support of Zionist militancy, lectured Ibn Saud about the British position in support of Zionism. But FDR died a few weeks after the meeting, and Ibn Saud, and other Arabs, would later lament the loss of an American president who was destined to do good for the Palestinians. Just as some Arabs still believe that John Kennedy, or later Richard Nixon, would have helped the Arabs if it were not for some Zionist conspiracies against him. But the meeting between Ibn Saud and Roosevelt was important, as it set the foundations for the long, solid relationship between the two very different countries.[424] The basics of the relationship were clear: the United States would explore and exploit Saudi crude—and would consequently have control over Saudi energy and foreign policy—in return for American protection of the royal family's rule. The royal family would provide the loyalty that it had provided to the British, and the fruits of the relationship would soon blossom when the two sides would work closely during the Cold War. Ibn Saud continued his close ties with the American government even after the death of his dear FDR.

Later on, Ibn Saud would exchange letters with Truman on the Palestinian problem, and Truman would only promise to look carefully into the matter. In one letter, Truman, after politely lecturing the Saudi king about the plight of the Jews (which is ironic given the recent discovery of documents showing the deep anti-Semitism of Truman[425]), assured Ibn Saud that "responsible Jewish leaders do not contemplate a policy of aggression against the Arab countries adjacent to Palestine."[426] After looking carefully, Truman, as is known, endorsed in full the Zionist position and ignored the aspirations and grievances of the indigenous Palestinians.[427] That, of course, did not disturb U.S.-Saudi relations. The king was getting a large supply of cash from the American oil companies, which in turn were getting far more cash from exploiting Saudi oil. The American recognition of Israel is said to have upset Prince Faysal, who was in New York arguing his government's position. But the king quickly got over his disappointment. When Iraq called on him to deprive the United States of oil, he reportedly said: "Give me $30 million and I'll join you."[428]

The relationship between the United States and Saudi Arabia continued to be close during the reign of King Saud.

The king made his first visit to the United States in 1957, and he almost caused a diplomatic crisis when he expressed reservations about landing in New York City, given the attacks on his person by New York City Mayor Robert Wagner, Jr., but he was persuaded to land in New York nevertheless.[429] Saud was like his father, or wanted desperately to emulate his father's lifestyle, especially in creating a very large family. He exceeded his father in the construction of ostentatious palaces. He learned an early lesson in dealing with the United States when in 1954 he tried to create his own tanker fleet; he was warned by the Americans, and after some dirty tricks, he surrendered the task to "a bidding" that, alas, went fair and square to none other than the American ARAMCO.[430] Saud had a conflict with the British in the early 1950s, when he laid claims to the Buraymi oasis on the borders with Oman, and after a failed arbitration, Saudi troops were expelled by a British-led force. It is noteworthy that ARAMCO had been responsible for the deployment of Saudi troops in the region.[431]

One cannot speak of Saud's relations with the United States without referring to his idiosyncratic fluctuations and political inconsistencies. At one point he was on Nasser's side but then conspired against him after Syria and Egypt entered a unitary union, creating what was known as the United Arab Republic. The head of security in the "northern region" (i.e., Syria) and its actual ruler, `Abdul-Hamid As-Sarraj, held a check given by King Saud to arrange for the assassination of Nasser. Yet after his abdication in favor of Faysal, the two maintained good relations. A state department report from the early period of Saud's rule noted his contradictory stances.[432] But Nasser was riding a high wave of popularity and assertiveness, having eliminated internal dissent from the left, the fundamentalist Islamists, and Colonel

Muhammad Najib, the first president of Egypt after the 1952 coup d'etat. Nasser's propaganda mocked the corruption of Saud, and conspiracies in the Gulf—including in Saudi Arabia—were laid at his doorstep. The threat of assassination and royal intrigue prodded the new king to create a praetorian guard that would later be known as the National Guard and that would be shaped and led by the current Crown Prince `Abdullah Bin `Abdul-`Aziz.

Nasser reached the peak of his power in 1956 when he nationalized the Suez Canal. This triggered the Tripartite Invasion of Egypt by the joining forces of Israel, France, and Britain. The invaders succeeded militarily, but instead of being toppled, Nasser emerged as the region-wide leader who would be compared to Saladin. President Eisenhower indirectly helped Nasser by forcing an Israeli withdrawal. He was not going to allow those defeated nations from World War II to prevail in his new sphere of influence. The Cold War did not permit adventures by U.S. allies unless they were calibrated and coordinated with the United States. Nasser swept the proverbial "Arab street"—a silly and derogatory reference to Arab public opinion. He was the leader who could do no wrong, the one who could stand up to Israel and the Western powers behind it. King Saud was aware of the magic of Nasser; he saw crowds greeting him in unprecedented fashion in Saudi Arabia. After the invasion of Egypt and the ensuing anti-Western sentiments that swept the region, the king cut off sale of oil to France and the UK. The Eisenhower Doctrine, which promised military and economic aid to countries engaged in the fight against communism, brought King Saud and other pro-Western Arab governments squarely into the American fold. That would seal the fate of Saudi Arabia as a linchpin of U.S. strategic posture in the Middle East and beyond. The Saudi government became the head of the "moderate camp"—moderate, in U.S. parlance, and "reactionary" in the eyes of its rivals—during the Cold War.

It was then that the United States began its coordination with Middle East governments (notably Iraq, Jordan, Lebanon, and Gulf governments) in an attempt to undermine the power of Nasser, and to persecute and oppress local progressive, socialist, communist, and Arab nationalist forces, all in the name of fighting communism. Those governments aligned themselves with the United States, not so much out of an ideological symmetry with Washington but because they were all unelected governments that suffered from lack of legitimacy, and they all felt the power of Nasser, which threatened the stability of these governments. Nasser's appeal affected even sectors in the armed forces of the government and senior members of the Saudi royal family.

It should also be added that in its fight against communism, the United States did not distinguish between the different ideological stripes: all those who were progressive in the slightest were placed in the enemy camp. Very much like the language of George W. Bush after 9-11 suggested, the United States was operating on the basis of a dogmatic adherence to a Manichean worldview: "You are either with us or against us." Toward that end the United States fought the Nonalignment Movement, although it comprised some countries that genuinely wanted to chart a course independent of both the United States and the Soviet Union. In fact, Nasser was not keen on placing his country fully and unconditionally in the Soviet camp; and his cultural preferences were clearly Western, but the unconditional support of the United States for Israel, and U.S. insistence on placing strict conditions on its sales of food and arms to Egypt, left Nasser with no choice.

The more the United States gave weapons to Israel, the more he drifted toward the Soviet Union, without even allowing for the operation of Egyptian communists, who were forced to dissolve themselves in 1964, after years of persecution at the hand of Nasser's regime.[433] And Nasser was never a fan of communism,[434] although U.S. propaganda at the time made him look like a communist menace.[435] In fact, former CIA Middle East expert Archie Roosevelt observed that one of the cardinal mistakes of U.S. Middle East policy was the official and fallacious conflation of communism and Arab nationalism.[436]

The American-Saudi alliance was officially set in the Saud-Eisenhower summit in 1957. Eisenhower drove to the airport to greet his guest, the first time he had ever done so.[437] Saud obtained a $180 million increase in U.S. military and economic aid—these were the days when Saudi Arabia received foreign aid—and the Americans obtained a five-year renewal of the U.S. Air Force base at Dhahran. Saud took his role as the head of the anticommunist camp in the Middle East seriously; he rushed troops to Jordan when the king felt threatened in April 1957.

But Saud, for purposes of internal rivalry with Faysal, was also susceptible to pressures from the progressive princes, Talal, Badr, and Mish`al. To them, he would deny that he was involved in the intrigues against Nasser that were being reported in the Syrian press. Furthermore, his incompetence, which was matched by his laziness, allowed the progressive technocrats, like the shrewd `Abdullah At-Tariqi, who was behind the founding of OPEC in 1960, to influence Saudi energy policy and its relationship with OPEC. And Prince Talal was pressuring Saud to allow for more openness and political participation. The United States must have been

alarmed at those developments and must have looked with
favor to the coup that brought Faysal to power, and which
ended the progressive Arab nationalist dreams of At-Tariqi.
Faysal had met Kennedy in 1962 in Washington and impressed
his hosts with his bitter anticommunism.

The era of Faysal elevated the U.S.-Saudi relationship
despite his musings regarding American bias in favor of Israel.
But he acted more hurt and disappointed than angry when discussing the U.S. position. And in his anti-Semitic outlook, it
was easy for him to explain the causes of American bias in
favor of Zionism. To trump Nasser's propaganda, King Faysal
put the émigré Muslim fundamentalist intellectuals from
Egypt to use in Saudi Arabia and beyond. Anticommunist literature spread in the region and was funded by the Saudi government, very likely with American participation. That the
most loyal anticommunists at the time were fundamentalist
Muslims did not bother the Americans. The fundamentalists
looked safe back then; they were not politically revolutionary,
and their use of violence was directed against the likes of
Nasser. That did not bother the Americans. The king helped
the effort by sponsoring and augmenting the powers of various outfits and organizations, all of which were meant to gather
Muslim states and organizations to rival the bloc of Nasser's
allies in the region.

Nasser had the support of public opinion, but Faysal had
multiple levels of support from Washington. But U.S. support
that was very visible or vocal for Faysal, in the context of the
1960s, was in fact damaging for the Saudis. Secrecy and covert-
ness were thus preferred. Against the juggernaut of Nasser's
propaganda apparatus, Faysal had the loyal backing of a
Lebanese publisher, Kamil Muruwwah, editor of *Al-Hayat*.
His newspaper was a daring voice of dissent against Nasser,

and Muruwwah knew how to package his message. He was such an irritant for Nasser and his supporters that Ibrahim Qulaylat, a local neighborhood tough guy and fanatical Nasser supporter, hired an assassin to eliminate Muruwwah.[438] And Faysal's feud with Nasser intensified after the 1962 coup in Yemen against the Royalist government; this triggered a savage war of proxies between Faysal and Nasser, where chemical weapons were used perhaps for the first time since World War I.

But the biggest problem for the United States in the Middle East was the unprecedented popularity of Nasser and the utter loathing that people felt toward the corruption and ostentation of the Gulf rulers. Stories of their sinful—by Islamic standards—indulgences filled the Arabic press, as did criticism of their dependence on the United States, which was as unpopular as it is today. Faysal and his fellow Gulf rulers were mocked and ridiculed by Nasser, and their reactionary form of Islam was compared unfavorably with the progressive and reformist Islam that Nasser was successfully pushing in Egypt and elsewhere. Nasser's version of "state feminism," as Mirvat Hatem has called it,[439] appealed to the left and to the thunderous Arab nationalist movement at the time. Faysal was still busy responding to international demands for the emancipation of slaves in Saudi Arabia.

The United States did not pressure Saudi Arabia. Then and now, the country was allowed to chart its own course and its own pace of reform, if that is what one can call it. Instead, the Saudi government was supported in crushing its dissent and in directing its energy policies away from the nationalist designs of some members of OPEC. Toward that end, Faysal designated his close advisor Shaykh Ahmad Zaki Al-Yamani, a close pro-American ally, to take over the oil policies and eradicate any thoughts of pro-Arab nationalism in the energy policy of the kingdom. In the intelligence sphere, he appointed his brother-in-law Kamal Adham, half-brother of Faysal's wife `Iffat. This corrupt dealer would make a fortune from commissions and from the tracts of lands that Faysal would award his close confidants. Adham was key in Saudi Arabia's pro-American orientation, and his role grew in the 1970s when he coordinated anti-Soviet policies with then-Egyptian president Sadat, when the latter was making an effort to win the favor of the Americans.

Faysal's efforts at expanding the American and Saudi spheres of influence were not successful at all. Wahhabiyyah's religious message was quite unappealing to Arabs and Muslims, and even more so was the pro-American alliance. Instead, Faysal would use his financial powers to reign in those pro-Western right-wing Muslim governments and to influence the media and popular culture through outright purchase of media outlets and publishing houses.

Faysal's big reprieve came in June 1967 when Nasser was severely wounded, politically speaking, by his devastating defeat in the Arab-Israeli War. Nasser was willing to forgive and forget provided he received the support that he needed to rebuild his destroyed armed forces. But the waning of Nasser's power was not the only factor convenient for Faysal and his pro-American intrigues. The 1967 defeat caused a wave of self-criticism and soul-searching throughout the Arab world. It also produced a revival of religion as a political force to be brandished against Israel, which used religion for its own cause.[440] The rejuvenation of religio-political movements received the immediate sponsorship from all those regimes who were intent on defeating the prevalent leftist and Arab nationalist forces, and that included Israel, Egypt (under

Anwar Sadat, who replaced Nasser after his death in 1970),
Jordan, and the Gulf regimes. The religious-oriented movement had the stamina and the resilience to combat leftist
and secular ideas, and they were trying to revive their credibility by harping on the responsibility of the leftist and Arab
nationalist forces for the Arab defeat.

That set the stage for King Faysal, with the support of the
Americans, to build an alliance of Islamic states and—most
important—Islamic nonstate actors who were incorporated
into the various leagues, associations, and organizations that
the Saudi government founded and funded throughout the
world. These were vehicles to spread Saudi propaganda and
to combat communist and leftist ideologies. Nasser was too
preoccupied with reconstruction of Egyptian armed forces to
interfere or worry about the Saudi campaign. Nasser's death
in 1970 ushered in the Saudi era, and the ascendancy of right-
wing forces and regimes. There were still some anti-American
voices among Arab officialdom: in the regimes of South
Yemen, Libya, Iraq, and Syria. But none of them posed a threat
to Saudi interests, and Saudi Arabia managed to co-opt the
most formidable of the rivals, namely Syria and Iraq. The
Saudi elite always used different princes for different mis-
sions; Crown Prince `Abdullah was used to appease the Syrian
regime, with which he was related by way of his marriage to
the leader's family.

But the real rise of American-Saudi relations emerged in
the Fahd era; Faysal was assassinated in 1975, and King Khalid,
who was more into his prayers, horses, and falcons than he
was into the affairs of the government, succeeded him. His
image was one of piety, which pleased the religious establishment, who did not respect Crown Prince Fahd. Fahd and his
Sudayri brothers positioned themselves in the government's

key posts, and King Khalid, who stuck to the ceremonial and symbolic dimensions of his job, did not threaten them. The Soviet invasion of Afghanistan coincided with the end of the Carter administration and the beginning of the Reagan administration. And in Arab politics, there has always been disquiet toward the Democratic Party and Democratic presidents in the United States, out of the myth that Jewish interests dominate the party. The Republicans, on the other hand, were looked at more favorably, up until the election of George W. Bush. *Al-Hayat* columnist Jihad Al-Khazin has regularly written about being in the office of the secretary-general, `Amru Musa, of the League of Arab States when news of George Bush's victory came. He describes the relief on the face of Musa.

The reasons for Arab preference for the Republican Party and Republican presidents are multifaceted. First, Arab governments are under the impression that the Republican Party—unlike the Democratic Party—is not controlled by Jewish interests. Second, the Republican Party is seen as having strong oil interests and connections, which are perceived to be friendly to Arab issues and causes. Third, many Arabs remember President Eisenhower's pressuring Israel to withdraw from Sinai in 1956 as an act of courage. Fourth, there is probably a view among the Saudi elite that Republican presidents are more macho and gutsy than the Democratic presidents who may bother Saudi Arabia if they invoke the issue of human rights, as Carter did, without, of course, becoming hostile in the slightest toward the Saudi regime while he was in power. In fact, this self-styled human rights president declared in 1977 that there "has not been any nation in the world that has been more cooperative than Saudi Arabia."[441] Carter was also, in his own words, "particularly proud in a personal way of [his] relationship with the Saudi leaders. This has been a very gratifying thing to me while I was President and the last two years since I left the White House."[442]

The presidency of Ronald Reagan and the Soviet invasion of Afghanistan created the golden opportunity for those in the Saudi government (Crown Prince Fahd; Prince Turki Bin Faysal, head of foreign intelligence; Prince Sultan Bin `Abdul-`Aziz, minister of defense; and Prince Bandar Bin Sultan, later Saudi ambassador to the United States) who had been pushing for the transformation of U.S.-Saudi relations to broaden their basis from energy to include such matters as covert operations and strategic cooperation. Prince Bandar was favored by his Uncle Fahd and set up shop in the United States. He led the fight for the sale of F-15 fighter jets to the kingdom in 1978 and the sale of AWACs in 1981. He was appointed ambassador in Washington, D.C., in 1983 and promoted to the rank of minister in 1995.[443] He is currently dean of the Diplomatic Corps in the American capital.

The Soviet invasion of Afghanistan opened a new chapter in U.S.-Saudi relations and joint covert operations. Prince Turki and Prince Bandar (both of whom had studied in the United States) constituted the pro-American lobby that was not satisfied with the level of U.S.-Saudi relations. They also wanted to try to replace Israel as a strategic partner for the United States in the Middle East. Bandar would set the stage in Washington by creating a pro-Saudi lobby through his contacts with business, media, Congress, and the White House, while Prince Turki would do the dirty work on the ground in Pakistan and Afghanistan to form an army of anticommunist forces—an army about which the United States preferred not to ask questions. The only credentials that were required were bitter anticommunism. The more anticommunist the better, they believed. The ones who fit the bill were the hardened Islamic fundamentalist rejects and roving fanatic revolutionaries who wanted to prove that Islam could defeat powerful enemies. They were also pragmatic enough to accept CIA money, weapons, and training.[444] This was the time when Bin Ladin came into prominence; he seems to have met every senior prince. Even Crown Prince `Abdullah now admits to having met him. "I met him once. He came to my house.... This was a long time ago, at the time of the Soviet invasion of Afghanistan in the 1980s," he told celebrity interviewer Barbara Walters.[445] Prince Turki had a more intimate knowledge of Bin Ladin. He admits that he had "met with him several times." And he remembers him "a relatively pleasant man, very shy, soft-spoken."[446] Bin Ladin became a key recruiter for the Saudi-American jihad cause.[447] And even the Saudi ambassador in Washington, D.C., Prince Bandar, admits to having met Bin Ladin.[448] Of course, to draw attention to the links between members of the Saudi elite and Bin Ladin is not to buy into the conspiracy theories that assert that Saudi Arabia was behind September 11 and behind Al-Qa`idah.[449] And it is important to note that we are now learning about the extent of the links between the higher echelons of the Saudi royal family and the Bin Ladin network during the Afghan war, but we have little knowledge of U.S. links to the Bin Ladin network in the 1990s.

The pro-American Saudi camp also wanted to help the American war on communism in places outside the Middle East. The public learned about the Saudi financing of the Contras, to the tune of millions of dollars, only because the Iran-Contra investigations revealed the Saudi role despite the Reagan administration's energetic effort to cover it up. Throughout, the Reagan administration would publicly refer to Saudi Arabia as an unnamed country.[450] Bob Woodward also refers to Saudi funding of U.S. covert operations in Lebanon.[451] We still do not know the extent to which Saudi-Lebanese billionaire Rafiq Hariri (current prime minister of Lebanon) coordinated Saudi-American covert operations, given his regional travels and alliance with Prince Bandar, especially during Saudi policy initiatives in the 1980s in the Middle East. Even Prince Turki had to admit that "Bandar operated outside the norm.... He conducted secret operations out of normal channels, with King Fahd's permission and blessing, that I was not aware of."[452] It was in this context that King Fahd assumed the throne in 1983 and could steer Saudi foreign policy according to his preferences, with little interference from either Saudi foreign minister, Saud Al-Faysal, or even his crown prince, ʿAbdullah. He entered the foreign policy scene in a major way when he announced his Fahd Plan of 1981, which was intended to facilitate American "peace" initiatives under Ronald Reagan. The Reagan plan of 1982 was close to Fahd's plan, although both wound up stillborn.

The Iraqi invasion of Kuwait strengthened King Fahd's hand and his vision of closer cooperation with the United States; but it also exposed the political and security vulnerabilities of his regime. It brought Crown Prince ʿAbdullah to his side as far as allowing the United States to deploy its troops in Saudi Arabia, despite the reservations that ʿAbdullah may have had at the time. American presence also favored the role of Prince Sultan, the minister of defense, who is a champion of close Saudi-American alliance. This also undermined the Saudi regime by augmenting the case of the opposition, be it liberal or fundamentalist. Prince Nayif, the minister of interior, admits: "Ever since the Gulf War of 1991, we are perceived in the Arab world as a pawn of the United States."[453]

The Saudi government was easily portrayed as an American protectorate. American policies in the Middle East, from continued American support of Israeli oppression, persecution, and killing of Palestinians (in addition to Clinton's exclusive sympathy for Israeli victims) to the American insistence on the unending prolongation of Iraqi sanctions, and the suffering of the Iraqi people, looked bad for American allies such as Saudi Arabia.

But King Fahd was largely—if not totally—excluded from power after his 1995 stroke. He was confined to a wheelchair and to royal decrees issued in his name. Crown Prince `Abdullah took over, and the relationship between the two countries continued to grow. President Clinton protected the kingdom when it came under attack from law enforcement agencies that criticized Saudi lack of cooperation in the investigation of the Khobar Towers bombing in 1996. When Bush took over, the Saudi elite had high hopes. The Bush family had close friendships with Saudi princes. And George W. Bush's father was the counterpart to Crown Prince `Abdullah when the former was vice president of the United States. Prince Bandar was personally close to the Bush family, and his wife was a friend of Barbara Bush. But George W. Bush was highly inexperienced in foreign policy. He relied on a group of advisors, many of whom were not enthusiastic champions of the Saudi government. What is commonly known as the neo-conservative sector of the administration seems to promote Israel, at the exclusion of all Arab countries, unless they— like Jordan—act according to Israeli wishes in the region. Saudi Arabia would not go as far as Jordan in pleasing Israeli demand.

Crown Prince `Abdullah was worried enough about the pro-Likud direction of the administration, and he drafted a letter to the American president in August 2001 warning against the United States' Middle East policy and stating that differences between the two countries had "grown so great."[454] `Abdullah postponed a scheduled trip to the United States, and former president George H. W. Bush telephoned the crown prince in the summer of 2001 to assure him that his son had the right feelings about Saudi Arabia. And his displeasure with the United States was intended to reflect Saudi public opinion, which had been unhappy with the United States.[455] September 11, 2001, of course, changed everything.

The Saudi government was quite nervous about the attacks; they subjected the Saudi government and country to close scrutiny by the U.S. Congress and press. The U.S. government consistently defended the Saudi royal family and played down its shortcomings and human rights violations. As loud as the United States was about spreading democracy in the Middle East, it remained silent about the Saudi dictatorship.[456] When Secretary of State Powell announced the $29 million project to spread democracy in the Arab world, he shielded Saudi Arabia. In a tough interview with *Al-Quds Al-`Arabi* in 2002, Powell stated: "I respect their culture and their heritage and their traditions…. It is not the role of the U.S. to dictate change…."[457] Those statements, of course, carry little credibility, and when quizzed further in the aforementioned interview, he abruptly ended the interview. Saudi Arabia is a thorny issue for U.S. foreign policy.

The kingdom acted nervously after September 11. Prince Nayif was in denial, refusing to admit that any Saudis were among the hijackers. He first blamed the Zionists for blaming Saudis, and then later blamed the Islamic Muslim Brotherhood for causing so much trouble for the kingdom. Perhaps he was referring to the fact that Saudi Arabia gave asylum to members and leaders of Muslim Brotherhood organizations from

Table 8.1

SAUDI PUBLIC OPINION ON A VARIETY OF ISSUES

Opinion/Position	Pct. (%)
Consider religion the number one concern in personal life	95[461]
Consider religious faith the number one value for children	96[462]
Consider the Palestine issue as number one issue of political importance	97[463]
Define "being Arab" as number one source of identity (ahead of religion)	86[464]
Unfavorable opinion of the United States	87[465]
Unfavorable opinion of Israel	97[466]
Favorable opinion of American people	43[467]
Favorable opinion of American science and technology	71[468]
Favorable opinion of American movies and TV	54[469]
Unfavorable opinion of U.S. policy toward Palestinians	90[470]
Unfavorable opinion of U.S. policy toward Arab nations	88[471]
Favorable opinion of U.S.-Iraq war of 1991	23[472]

different Arab countries and allowed them to spread their message, and even teach at Saudi schools and universities. The clerical establishment condemned the attacks but did not act defensively.[458] The Saudi public clearly expressed protest against the United States and Israel—largely because it is permitted. There are some reports of Saudi sympathy for Bin Ladin (one Saudi writer even talked of some Saudis "gloating"[459] over U.S. tragedy), but that is much harder to document.[460] Existing public opinion surveys conducted in Saudi Arabia after September 11 indicate that there is indeed a gap between the government policies and the public mood in the kingdom. Table 7.1 shows some of the findings of such surveys conducted in the kingdom after September 11.

This clearly suggests that the Saudi government and the Saudi public are not on the same side, regardless of whether that side is liberal or fundamentalist. The gap between the two sides was not narrowed in February 2002 when Crown Prince `Abdullah announced his famous initiative, which became known as Crown Prince `Abdullah's initiative, after meeting with Thomas Friedman, who is unpopular in the Middle East for his insulting *New York Times* articles against Arabs, his advocacy of a civil war "within Islam," and his endorsement of Israeli positions. Crown Prince `Abdullah's initiative entailed an official Arab pledge for full normalization of relations with Israel, in return for full Israeli withdrawal from the Arab territories occupied in 1967. The initiative was endorsed by the Arab summit a month later, but `Abdullah had to twist some arms to win approval.[473] A few days later the Sharon government ordered an invasion of the West Bank, and the massacres (American and Israeli officials argue that what happened in the Jenin Camp was not technically a massacre because no more than fifty-six

Palestinians were killed) that ensued placed the crown prince in an awkward position. He could not defend himself vis-à-vis Arab public opinion. He largely remained silent, the few public statements issued in his name notwithstanding. Instead, a group of some of the most well-known Saudi intellectuals signed a petition in which they expressed strong support for the Palestinians and demanded an Arab response to the "American-Israeli penetration" of the Arab states.[474]

The crown prince also reversed his earlier position regarding not visiting the United States, which he had said he would not do, given U.S. support for Sharon. The crisis in U.S.-Saudi relations led him to visit President George Bush's farm in Texas. The summit between the two leaders was, by most accounts, a diplomatic disaster.[475] There were several cultural faux pas, the biggest of which was that the American president held `Abdullah's hands and led him in Christian prayer. Diplomatically, not much was achieved despite warm statements here and there. The crown prince, to his Saudi audience, took credit for Bush's utterance of the word "Palestine."[476] The issuance of the congressional report in July 2003 on the September 11 attacks did not help things.[477] In that report there were rumored to be numerous revealing statements excised by U.S. authorities regarding Saudi complicity and involvement, especially in the funding of the Al-Qa`idah network. This led to a sudden visit by Foreign Minister Sa`ud Al-Faysal to Washington to urge the president to release the section of the report that dealt with Saudi Arabia.[478] The president refused on grounds of national security, but the media storm did not subside. It was clear that the president did not want to reveal some embarrassing details that may prove to cause further damage to the image of the Saudi royal family in the U.S. press, while the press continued to attack the White House for its reluctance to reveal information dealing with Saudi financial ties to terrorism.

The Saudi family replied primarily in two ways. The first was to launch a propaganda campaign in the United States to reach out to the American public and Congress. The national security advisor of the crown prince, the ubiquitous `Adil Al-Jubayr,[479] set up shop in Washington to manage the Saudi propaganda campaign. The Saudi government spent millions on its public relations, just as Israel was spending millions on its U.S. propaganda after the eruption of the Palestinian intifada in September 2000.[480] To guarantee favorable coverage, the Saudi government hired a "slew of DC's most powerful lobbying and PR firms—including turning to an ad-buying company that's helped top Republicans—to buff its post-9/11 image."[481] One powerful firm, Patton Boggs, received a fee of $100,000 every two months, while Qorvis Communications received $200,000 per month.[482] However, the Saudi propaganda campaign does not seem to have helped, especially since Arab money is always seen as controversial. Israel, which spends millions on its U.S. propaganda, does not get the scrutiny that Saudi expenditure gets in the U.S. media. There are also pro-Israeli journalists who speak about Saudi Arabia and Arab influence in the same way that anti-Semites speak about Jewish influence.[483]

And in 2004, U.S.-Saudi relations seem to reflect a schizophrenic nature; on the one hand, the White House continues to insist on a very close relationship with the Saudi royal family, and the administration is keen on protecting the image and interests of Saudi Arabia in the United States. On the other hand, the press and the public in the United States continue to identify Saudi Arabia as a potential enemy and raise questions about Saudi ties to terrorism. It is of course highly noteworthy that the American press never paid much attention to Saudi violations of human rights prior to 9-11. It is as if the press suddenly got word that there is severe oppression in Saudi Arabia. It should also be mentioned that the influential pro-Israeli lobby in Washington is very adamant in attacking all Arab governments that do not sign peace treaties with Israel. Thus, the Jordanian government, which cooperates with Israel on more than one level, and which consistently violates the human rights of citizens, is shielded from congressional and media attacks. This may explain why many Arab governments (Morocco, Libya, UAE, Oman, and Qatar) that did not have land disputes with Israel have entered into secret and public negotiations with Israel based on the belief that such measures would enhance their standing in the United States. U.S.-Saudi relations will continue to reflect the asymmetry between official and public perceptions of the Saudi royal family. Saudi Arabia will continue its difficult efforts to appease divergent constituencies in Washington, D.C., and in Saudi Arabia. At this point, the royal family appears more concerned about its American constituency than about its domestic audience. It is highly likely that it will be unable to continue pleasing both camps simultaneously; one of the two sides will eventually break with the royal family.

Conclusion

Events are moving fast in Saudi Arabia. Violence has been escalating. Armed fights and raids are being reported in the streets of Riyadh, in the holy city of Mecca, and elsewhere in the kingdom. Saudi Arabia now wants the world to believe that it has entered into the throes of the war on terrorism. Of course, terrorism is real, but it is difficult to trust declarations by states that have themselves engaged in acts of violence against civilians.

Saudi Arabia is more nervous than ever. U.S.-Saudi relations may become a national issue in the lead-up to the U.S. presidential elections, and that would bring to the Saudis embarrassing attention that it has tried hard to avoid. Democratic presidential candidate John Kerry, who has hitherto failed to inspire even the Democratic Party stalwarts, has added his voice to those criticizing Saudi Arabia, although he has been silent for decades about Saudi violations of human rights. He is not alone, of course. American hypocrisy on Saudi issues cuts across party lines. Kerry emphatically yelled in December 2003: "We need to see the new textbooks. We need to hear what the government-financed clerics are preaching."[484] The kingdom is taking these signs very seriously. Its flamboyant ambassador in Washington has been largely silenced by the team of Crown Prince `Abdullah, which relies on the services of much less assertive spokesmen. And in typical Saudi fashion, money is spent generously to bolster the image of the seemingly dysfunctional royal family. According to Justice Department records, the Saudis have spent some $17.6 million since the September 11 attacks.[485] In one two-week period after the attacks, some 1,541 Saudi ads ran on American television. There is no evidence that this propaganda campaign has borne fruit for the royal family. And in their propaganda efforts, the royal family can count on the services and assistance of influential Americans, especially those who were part of the administration of George H. W. Bush, who continued to do work with the Saudi government after his retirement. Bush receives between $80,000 and $100,000 for each speech he makes for the Carlyle Group. He also gets undisclosed payments.[486] In fact, a number of influential Republicans, including James A. Baker, Dick Darman, and Frank Carlucci, have been hired by the powerful Carlyle Group, which does a lot of work in Saudi Arabia.[487] Among the clients of the Carlyle Group are (or were) Prince Al-Walid Bin Talal, the Bin Ladin family, and George Soros.[488]

Domestically, the royal family is hitting hard, not only against those who are resorting to vicious acts of terrorism but also against any manifestation of dissent. Thus, when tens of people in Saudi Arabia responded in October 2003 to calls issued by Saudi dissident Sa`d Al-Faqih in London for demonstrations in support of political and social reform, the minister of interior hit them hard. He bluntly declared that "gatherings and demonstrations are contrary to what is established [sic]."[489] And his ministry proudly announced that those gatherings were dealt with by security forces according "to the security obligation."[490] Such activities, added a source in the ministry, are inconsistent with "our Islamic values and mores."[491] The religious elite of the kingdom have been standing in support of the government in the last few years. The mufti of the kingdom, `Abdul-`Aziz Al-Ash-Shaykh (a descendant of Muhammad Ibn `Abdul-Wahab), declared that demonstrations are "mere chaos and are not part of Muslim morals." He added that demonstrators constitute "a deviant group of no consideration, and people who have spoiled perception and little awareness."[492]

The government also cracked down on the religious structure of the kingdom, which may become the most costly political move for the royal family. In late 2003, the government suspended some seventeen hundred preachers, Imams, and callers to prayer—some were fired and others were sent for reeducation courses.[493] The government kept repeating its messages of moderation in the interpretation of Islam; but that, of course, clashes with the very ideology on which the kingdom was founded and which serves as the bond between the royal family and the clerical establishment of the House of Shaykh.

Crown Prince `Abdullah also introduced some token formal measures to align himself with the cause of reform that would please the United States but displease the Wahhabiyyah constituency. The Saudi crisis of legitimacy may in fact deepen. The government has responded to 9-11 with discourse of reform, and with compliance with U.S. demands for pressures on the Palestinian national movement. Yet the militant youth of the kingdom—the ones who seem to have rallied in support of Al-Qa`idah—may find more reasons for their rebellion. The crown prince, in fact, made a call for reform in the Arab world in general in January 2003, perhaps to deny that the kingdom was experiencing any special stress. And the recent string of bombings in the kingdom led the government to rush through some other verbal promises of reform. In October 2003, the king of Saudi Arabia announced—or we should say it was announced that the king has announced, as he remains largely severely debilitated—that from now on the Shura Council, the advisory body that has no binding authority, would be able to initiate legislation.[494] But that measure is less impressive than it sounds because the council would then forward their proposals—and they are just proposals—to the king, and he alone would decide whether they would be adopted or discarded. This came weeks after another announcement regarding holding municipal elections in the kingdom in 2004. But that too is meaningless, as the process of free elections and contestations in the kingdom does not exist. In fact, the kingdom's security environment, especially after the massive residential bombings in May and October 2003, has deteriorated substantially. The bombings have revealed the degree of militant presence within the kingdom, and the level of Saudi police vulnerabilities.

The debate in the kingdom continues. Given the restrictions on foreign press access, and the absence of an open domestic media, one can only speak about developments in the kingdom with caution. But it is clear that one can distinguish between the Shi`ite sector and the Sunni sector. The Shi`ite sector of the population seems always to get energized in reaction to developments outside the kingdom. The rejuvenation of Shi`ite power in Saudi Arabia following the Iranian revolution in 1979 was met with repression and intolerance, symptomatic of the Wahhabi attitude toward Shi`ism. The war in Iraq and the rise of Shi`ite power in Saudi Arabia's neighbor may also add to the political demands of Saudi Shi`ites for more equality and fairness in the kingdom and for the simple right to religious worship. But the Shi`ites cannot by definition join with the dissident militant Wahhabi movement that questions their very commitment to Islam. More likely, the Shi`ites will join forces with the reformers in the Sunni population.

Not much is known about the reformists in the kingdom and whether they have any social basis of support. But it has become clear that the rise of liberal-reformist voices in the Saudi media has been orchestrated by the crown prince. And when those voices deviate too much from the charted course or when they provoke the religious establishment, they can easily be discarded, as happened to Jamal Al-Khajuqji, who was fired after using his newspaper *Al-Watan* to mock the clergy. The crown prince may also be using the reformist professional class in order to prepare for the crucial succession struggle with his half-brothers that will commence when the king passes away. This may explain why the Sudayri Seven have been largely absent or silent, and why even the vocal pro-American Prince Sultan, minister of defense, has not been vocal in defending U.S.-Saudi relations since 9-11. If anything, he has in fact spoken against the U.S. war in Afghanistan and against U.S. policy in support of Israel.

The royal family may be facing the most serious threat to its very existence since the founding of the kingdom, certainly since the death of the founder, King `Abdul-`Aziz. Its relations with the United States, which sheltered it in the past, are now insufficient to provide a sense of security to the Saudi rulers. The announced withdrawal of U.S. troops may have indirectly emboldened the violent opposition movement and increased the vulnerability of the family. The family has to decide where its fortunes and destiny lie, whether in a stronger alliance with the United States or in a continued position deeply rooted within Islamic ideology and secrecy. The utilization of Wahhabi ideology as the source of political legitimacy for the kingdom has served the stability of Saudi rule, but it has come at a price: the alienation of sectors in Western society after 9-11 and the demoralization of the professional reformer section of Saudi society. This conflict will inevitably be reflected in the struggle for power within the royal family, a struggle that proceeds in earnest even though King Fahd remains the official monarch.

Bush has his own dilemmas too. He regularly declares his friendship with the Saudi government but utters not a single word of meaningful criticism. Some speak of close family ties between Bin Ladin's family and the Bush family, and that fuels conspiracy theories on both sides of the Atlantic. It is not fair to draw conclusions about an association between the Bin Ladin family members in Texas (who did not have any political ties to their estranged family member Usamah) and the Bush family in order to construct some conspiracy theory about September 11, as the French journalist Eric Laurent has done in his *La guerre des Bush : Les secrets inavouables d'un conflit*,[495] or even the popular Michael Moore in his recent best seller.[496] The association between the Saudi royal family and the United States is not familial but institutional, between the Saudi government and the successive American administrations. Not a single American administration dared to speak about the abysmal human rights conditions in the kingdom. If anything, the White House has historically served to shield the royal family from press and occasional congressional criticisms—something the Bush administration has gone out of its way to do. Congress has become vocal in its criticism of Saudi Arabia but not necessarily out of concern for human rights. Under the influence of the pro-Israel lobby, members of Congress have in fact been critical of every single Arab country. But if an Arab country makes peace with Israel—as Egypt and Jordan did—their human rights violations will be overlooked and their requests for arms purchases will be met. Even Egypt has been receiving some criticisms from Congress but only because it has not been very warm toward Israel. So the prevailing criteria are not about human rights and dignity but about serving the United States and its core interests, including Israel. Thus Thomas Friedman has recently indicated that all will be well in Saudi Arabia if only the royal family cooperates with Israel.[497]

September 11 has perhaps caused irreparable damage to U.S.–Saudi relations, if not at the official level then certainly at the public level. Extremist ideas, consistent with Wahhabi socialization, are spreading among Saudi youth, and the American public has easily succumbed to the demonization of all things Islamic and Arab. The prospects for the Saudi royals' survival remain uncertain, and official American protection of their political control is of little use against the decentralized, asymmetrical forces that threaten them. The issuance of an unprecedented petition in December 2003, in which Saudi signatories called for the establishment of a constitutional monarchy,[498] only underlines the precariousness of the rule of the House of Saud and the increasing verve of Saudi opposition. But those who are opposed to reform are also regrouping; writers, intellectuals, and clerics presented a petition in late 2003 calling on the government to resist calls for curricular reforms. But the government is incapable of reforming a system that is so corrupt and ancient. The intentions of the royal family were made clear in March 2004 when Prince Sultan ruled out the idea of elections for the members of the powerless Shura Council because he said that unedu-

cated and illiterate people may get elected.[499] This is in a kingdom where the king and the crown prince are themselves
barely literate.

The turmoil in the kingdom, in Saudi society, and in the
royal family, is too deep to be reduced to a conflict between two
brothers.[500] The House of Saud was an unnatural phenomenon that has prevailed for so long due to enormous wealth and
to the protection of powerful allies. If the House of Saud is to
fall, it is difficult to know if underlying social forces, so long
suppressed, may finally roil to the surface. That prospect does
not necessarily bode ill for the people of Saudi Arabia, unless
an equally intolerant and oppressive alternative takes over.

Unfortunately, the escalating violence, including the massive suicide bombing outside the headquarters of the Saudi
traffic authority in Riyadh in April 2004, indicates the serious-
ness, determination, and resilience of those committed to
such an alternative. The militant network that received the
government largesse during the war in Afghanistan, is driving
its bomb-laden vehicles toward its former benefactors—the
United States and the House of Saud.

In Richard Clarke's new book, *Against All Enemies*, we
learn that the Saudi relationship with Bin Ladin was more
extensive than had previously been revealed. Prince Turki had
apparently recruited Bin Ladin and his network for some
unidentified "covert operations" against the leftist regime in
the (former) South Yemen. Predictably, the Saudi government
responded to Clark's revelations with clumsiness, bravado,
and false declarations and statements. Saudi Minister of
Defense Prince Sultan now declares that 80 percent of all
Saudi terrorists have been eliminated. They want to convince
the world and themselves that all is well. But all is not well.
All has been getting worse.

Saudi-American relations remain close. Bob Woodward's new book, *Plan of Attack*, reveals that the Saudi ambassador in D.C., Prince Bandar, continues to enjoy unusual access to the Oval Office. Woodward reports that Prince Bandar received Iraq war plans before Colin Powell. It is unlikely that the White House will diverge from the standard U.S. policy of protection for the House of Saud after the November 2004 elections, regardless of who wins.

In duping the U.S. public to go to war, neo-conservatives in Washington promised that regime change in Iraq would change the Middle East forever. They talked about restructuring the region. As we now know, they were wrong in all of their assumptions and predictions except one: they have in fact changed the region forever. But instead of liberating a people into democracy, the U.S. invasion and occupation of Iraq has energized insurgent outrage, militancy, recruitment, and organizing. Fanatical and radical forces are spreading, and their lethal and destabilizing impact threatens not only Iraq and America's favorite royal dictatorship but Europe and beyond.

Notes

1.   Amnesty International, *Report 2003* (New York: Amnesty International, 2003), 213.
2.   Chicago Council on Foreign Relations and the German Marshall Fund of the U.S., *Worldviews 2002* (Chicago: Chicago Council on Foreign Relations, October 2002), 70.
3.   *Times* (London), August 28, 2002.
4.   Joseph Persico, *Casey: From the OSS to the CIA* (New York: Viking, 1990).
5.   Bob Woodward, *Veil: The Secret World of the CIA* (New York: Simon and Schuster, 1987). Woodward maintains that Saudi Arabia funded American efforts against "terrorism" in Lebanon, which included a car bomb that killed scores of innocent people but missed its aim, a Shi`ite cleric.
6.   For the record of U.S. alliance with Saddam Husayn, see the files of the National Security Archives at: www.gwu.edu/~nsarchiv/special/iraq/index.htm.
7.   The full text can be found at: new.globalfreepress.com/911/fullreport/pages/001.shtml. The report has some twenty-eight pages of censored information dealing mostly with Saudi Arabia. See the *New York Times*, July 26, 2003, A1.
8.   See the comments of Prince Saud in *Al-Hayat*, August 7, 2003.
9.   *Time*, September 1, 2003.
10. See *Ash-Sharq Al-Awsat*, August 26, 2003, 1.
11. Malcom Kerr, *The Arab Cold War: Gamal Abd Al-Nasir and His Rivals, 1858–1970* (New York: Oxford University Press, 1971).
12. A good record of this movement can be found in the series of interviews by Al-Jazeera TV with Prince Talal in December 2000. See the transcripts at www.aljazeera.net/programs/century_witness/articles/ 2000/12/12-17-2.htm.
13. See "Saudi Arabia, 2003 Report," Human Rights Watch www.hrw.org/wr2k3/mideast6.html
14. Communication with Munif's son, Yasir.
15. Nezar Qabbani, *Qasa'id Maghdub `Alayha* (Resented Poems) (Beirut: Manshurat Nezar Qabbani, 1992), 85–86.
16. This is based on a conversation with the owner of the newspaper in 1993.

17. See the list in *Al-Hayat*, August 16, 2003.

18. Sandra Mackey, *The Saudis* (Boston: Houghton Mifflin Company, 1987).

19. Ibid., 154. The author called Mackey after the publication of her book and bluntly asked about her source of information on this, given its private nature. She simply said: "Oh, everybody knows that."

20. Ibid., 193.

21. Ibid., 77.

22. Ibid., 152.

23. Robert Lacey, *The Kingdom: Arabia & the House of Saud* (New York: Avon Books, 1981), 271.

24. Douglas F. Graham, *Saudi Arabia Unveiled* (Dubuque, Iowa: Hunt Publishing, 1991), 79. The author also adheres to the cliché that religion determines all. It should be noted that none other than former national security advisor in the Carter administration, Zbigniew Brzezinski, endorsed the book.

25. Stephen Schwartz, *The Two Faces of Islam: The House of Saud from Tradition to Terror* (New York: Doubleday, 2002), 107. The author is not trained in Middle East studies or in Islam, although he brags that he is "bilingual in English and Spanish." See p. xvi.

26. Kamal Salibi, *A History of Arabia* (Delmar, N.Y.: Caravan, 1980), 1.

27. Hafidh Wahbah, *Jazirat Al-`Arab fi-l-Qarn Al-`Ishrin* (Arabia in the Twentieth Century) (Cairo: Maktabat An-Nahdah, 1961), 1.

28. Salibi, *A History of Arabia*, 8.

29. Wahbah, *Jazirat Al-`Arab*, 112.

30. Raphael Patai, *The Arab Mind* (New York: Scribner's Sons, 1973). In response to academic critiques of his book, in later editions Patai insisted that only PLO apologists were displeased with his book. See the 1983 revised edition, p. ix.

31. Waddah Shararah, *Al-Ahl wa-l-Ghanimah: Muqawwimat As-Siyasah fi-l-Mamlaka-l-`Arabiyya-s-Sa`udiyyah* (The Folks and the Booty: The Foundations of Politics in the Saudi Arabian Kingdom) (Beirut: Dar At-Tali`ah, 1981).

32. Ira Lapidus, "Tribes and State Formation in Islamic History," in *Tribes and State Formation in the Middle East*, eds. Philip Khoury and Joseph Kostiner (Berkeley, Calif.: University of California Press, 1990), 26.

33. Benedict Anderson, *Imagined Communities: Reflections on the Origin and Spread of Nations*, rev. ed. (New York: Verso, 1991).

34. See Joseph Kostiner, "Transforming Dualities: Tribe and State Formation in Saudi Arabia," in *Tribes and State Formation in the Middle East*, eds. Philip Khoury and Joseph Kostiner (Berkeley, Calif.: University of California Press, 1990), 228.

35. See Kostiner, "Transforming Dualities," 226.

36. David Lamb, *The Arabs: Journeys Beyond the Mirage* (New York: Random House, 1987).

37. See Kostiner, "Transforming Dualities," 244.

38. Peter Theroux has competently translated into English the first volume of the five-volume novel. See Abdelrahman Munif, *Cities of Salt: A Novel* (New York: Random House, 1987). The Arab edition has been published

by Al-Mu'assasah Al-`Arabiyyah Li-d-Dirasat wa-n-Nashr in Beirut. Even in Saudi Arabia, where the book was banned, pirated copies have been published and circulated. The Saudi government has stripped the author of his citizenship.

39.   A.L. (de Corancez, Alexandre Olivier de Corancez), *Histoire des Wahabis, Depuis Leur Origine Jusqu'a la Fin de 1809* (Paris: Carpart, 1810).

40.   Ibid., 1.

41.   A high government official in Qatar told this writer in February 2004 that Qatar remains committed to Wahhabiyyah but that Saudi Wahhabiyyah is a corrupt version of the true Wahhabiyyah.

42.   The classic study remains Elizabeth Monroe, *Philby of Arabia* (London: Faber and Faber, 1973). As is well known, Philby profited from his relationship with King `Abdul-`Aziz, both directly and indirectly.

43.   From an opinion of Ibn Baz, posted on his official Web site: www.ibnbaz.org.sa/last_resault.asp?hID=719.

44.   See the interview in *Ukadh*, November 18, 2001.

45,   See his statement in *Al-Hayat*, July 2, 2003, 1.

46.   `Uthman bin `Abdullah Bin Bishr, *`Unwan Al-Majd fi Tarikh Majd* (The Title of Glory in the History of Najd) (Riyadh: Dar Al-`Abib, 1999), 8. The author, without any evidence, maintains that `Abdul-Wahab studied philosophy in Hamadan, Qum, and Isfahan.

47.   See Hamid Algar, *Wahhabism: A Critical Essay* (Oneonta, N.Y.: Islamic Publications International, 2002). This informative essay by a recognized scholar of Islam contains rare criticisms of Wahhabiyyah from a non-Orientalist perspective. But the author could not restrain himself from throwing polemical darts at his "enemies."

48.   See Amin Rihani, *Tarikh Najd Al-Hadith Wa Mulhaqatihi* (History of Najd and Its Annexations) (Beirut: Dar Sadir, 1928), 27.

49.   Muhammad Abu Zahrah, *Ibn Taymiyyah: Hayatuhu, `Asruhu, Ara'uhu, wa Fiqhuhu* (Ibn Taymiyyah: His Life, Age, Opinions, and Jurisprudence) (Cairo: Dar Al-Fikr Al-`Arabi, 1952).

50.   Algar, *Wahhabism*, 9.

51.   Rihani, *Tarikh Najd*, 38. Ahmad Ibn Hanbal is a founder of the most strict and conservative school of the four Sunni schools of jurisprudence. It was named after him.

52.   As quoted in `Aziz Al-`Adhmah, *Ibn Taymiyyah* (Beirut: Riad El-Rayyes Books, 2000), 21.

53.   See Elie A. Salem, *Political Theory and Institutions of the Khawarij*, (Baltimore, Md.: Johns Hopkins University Press, 1956).

54.   In an audiotape by Usamah Bin Ladin released on January 4, 2004, he lambasted Arab governments for persecuting Muslim "holy warriors" and dismissing them as "khawarij." From the tape as aired on Al-Jazeera TV on January 4, 2004.

55.   Melhem Chokr, *Zandaqa et Zindiqs en Islam au second siecle de l'hegire* (Damas: Institut Francais de Damas, 1993), 9.

56.   Unattributed saying cited in `Abdul-`Aziz Al-Muraghi, *Ibn Taymiyyah* (Cairo: Dar Ihya' Al-Kutub Al-`Arabiyyah, 1945), 70.

57. Ibn Taymiyyah, *Majmu`at Al-Fatawa* (The Collected Fatwas), vol. 28, eds. `Amir Al-Jazzar and Anwar Al-Baz (Al-Mansurah: Dar Al-Wafa', 1997), 274.
58. Ibid., 20.
59. Sa'ib `Abdul-Hamid, *Ibn Taymiyyah: Hayatuhu…`Aqa'iduhu* (Ibn Taymiyyah: His Life…Doctrines) (Beirut: Makaz Al-Ghadir li-d-Dirasat al-Islamiyyah, 1994).
60. Ibid., p. 153.
61. Algar, *Wahhabism,* 10.
62. Ibid., 180.
63. Henri Laoust, *Essaie sur les Doctrines Sociales et politiques de Taki-d-Din Ahmad Ibn Taymiya,* (Le Caire, 1939).
64. Ibid., 27.
65. Ibid.
66. `Abdul-`Aziz Bin Baz, *Muhammad `Ibn `Abdul-Wahab: Da`watuhu wa Siratuhu* (His Message and Biogrpahy) (Jiddah: Ad-Dar As-Sa`udiyyah, 1970), 21.
67. Ahmad Ibn Zayni Dahlan, *Al-Futuhat Al-Islamiyyah* (Islamic Conquests), vol. 2 (Cairo: Mu'assasat Al-`Alabi, 1968), 234–35.
68. Bin Bishr, *`Unwan Al-Majd,* 8.
69. Algar, *Wahhabism,* 6.
70. Bin Baz, *Muhammad `Ibn `Abdul-Wahab,* 22.
71. Bin Bishr, *`Unwan Al-Majd,* 7.
72. Rihani, *Tarikh Najd,* 29.
73. Ibid., 31.
74. `Aziz Al-`Adhmah, *Muhammad Bin `Abdul-Wahab* (Beirut: Riyad El-Rayyes, 2000), 11.
75. Algar, *Wahhabism,* 31.
76. See the excellent summary given in ibid., 31.
77. Muhammad `Abdul-Wahab, *Kitab At-Tawhid* (Book of Tawhid), cited in `Aziz Al-`Adhmah, *Muhammad,* 23.
78. "Benevolent predecessors" refers to the first generation of Muslims, Muhammad and his companions, who—we are told—lived the exemplary Muslim life, which ought to be emulated.
79. See *Kitab At-Tawhid,* in Rashid Rida, *Majmu`at At-Tawhid* (Cairo: Dar Al-Manar, A.H. 1346), 2; also cited in `Aziz Al-`Adhmah, *Muhammad,* 19.
80. *Kitab At-Tawhid,* 12.
81. Algar, *Wahhabism,* 34.
82. Qur'an, Surat An-Nisa', Ayat 116.
83. Husayn Ibn Ghannam, *Tarikh Najd,* (Beirut: Dar Ash-Shuruq, 1994), 108.
84. Sulayman `Abdul-Wahab, *As-Sawa`iq Al-Ilahiyyah fi-r-Radd `Ala-l-Wahhbiyyah* (Divine Thunderbolts in Replying to Wahhabism), ed. As-Sarawi (Beirut: Dar Dhu-l-Fiqar, 1997), 31–41.
85. Ibid., 42.
86. Ibid., 43.
87. Ibid.

88. Muhammad `Abdul-Wahab, "*Kashf Ash-Shubuhat,*" as cited in Ahmad Al-Katib, *Al-Fikr As-Siyasi Al-Wahhabi: Qira'ah Tahliliyyah* (Wahhabi Political Thought: An Analytical Reading) (London: Dar Ash-Shura, 2003), 24.

89. As cited in Ibn Ghannam, *Tarikh Najd,* 470–71.

90. Ibid., 353.

91. Ibid., 270–71.

92. `Abdul-`Aziz Al-`Abdul-Latif, *Da`awa Al-Munawa'in li-Da`wat Ash-Shaykh Muhammad Ibn `Abdul-Wahab* (The Cases Against the Case of Shaykh Muhammad Ibn `Abdul-Wahab) (Riyadh: Dar Al-Watan, A.H. 1412), 163.

93. On this see Maxime Rodinson, *Islam et capitalisme* (Paris: Editions du Seuil, 1966).

94. Ahmad Al-Husayn, *Da`wat Al-Imam Muhammad Ibn `Abdul-Wahab: Salafiyyah la Wahabiyyah* (The Call of Imam Muhammad Ibn `Abdul-Wahab: Salafiyyah not Wahabiyyah) (Riyadh: Dar `Alam Al-Kutub, 1999), 49.

95. Ibn Taymiyyah, *Majmu`at,* vol. 4, 450–52.

96. See Ahmad ibn Zayni Dahlan, *Ad-Durar As-Saniyyah fi-l-Ajwibah An-Najdiyyah* (Riyadh: Dar Al-Ifta', 1964), 30, 33.

97. Excerpts of his statement appear in *Al-Hayat,* August 22, 2003, 1.

98. Algar, *Wahhabism,* 35.

99. That is how it is defined in the definitive Ibn Mandhur, *Lisan Al-`Arab.*

100. Muhammad `Awad Al-Khatib,, *Al-Wahhabiyyah: Fikran wa Mumarasah* (Wahhabism: In Thought and Practice) (n.p.: Al-Mi`raj, 2000), 142–52.

101. Algar, *Wahhabism,* 35.

102. Rihani, *Tarikh Najd,* 33.

103. This date is given in Algar, *Wahhabism,* 23.

104. Bin Bishr, *`Unwan Al-Majd,* 257–58. The author reproduced the excellent translation of Hamid Algar in Algar, *Wahhabism,* 24–25.

105. `Abdul-`Aziz Tuwayjiri, *Li Surat Al-Layl Hatafa As-Sabah* (Beirut: Riad El-Rayyes, 1997), 46.

106. Ahmad Dahlan, *Al-Futuhat Al-Islamiyyah,* vol. 1, 314.

107. Wahbah, *Jazirat Al-`Arab,* 233.

108. Ibid., 234.

109. Ibid., 228.

110. Ibid., 227.

111. Husayn Khaz`al, *Tarikh Al-Jazirah Al-`Arabiyyah fi `Asr Muhammad Ibn `Abdul-Wahab* (History of Arabia During the Epoch of Muhammad Ibn `Abdul-Wahab) (Beirut: Dar Al-Kutub, 1973).

112. In religious leadership, Muhammad Ibn `Abdul-Wahab was succeeded by his sons `Abdullah and Hasan, and then `Abdur-Rahman, and later his son `Abdul-Latif and his son `Abdullah, after whom came Muhammad Bin `Abdul-Latif, followed by Muhammad Bin Ibrahim. See Anwar `Abdullah, *Al-`Ulama' Wa-l-`Arsh* (Clerics and the Throne) (London: 2000), 346.

113. The text of the letter, which is dated December 29, 1994, is posted on www.alwahabiya.org/articles/binladen_to_binbaz.htm.

114. Ibid.

115. The fatwa was printed in Salih Al-Wardani, *Ibn Baz: Faqih Al-Sa`ud* (Ibn Baz: The Cleric of the House of Saud) (Cairo: Dar Al-Husam, 1998), 121.

116. Ibn Baz, *Al-Jawab Al-Mufid fi Hukm At-Taswir* (The Useful Reply to the Ruling of Photography) (Jiddah: Dar Al-Mujtama`, 1987).

117. See Salih Al-Wardani, *Fatawa Ibn Baz* (The Fatwas of Ibn Baz) (Cairo: Dar Al-Hadaf, 1999), 112.

118. Al-Wardani, *Ibn Baz*, 119–20.

119. Fatwa no. 1653, August 22, A.H. 1397, cited in ibid., 133.

120. See his fatwa, signed by other members of the Permanent Committee, in Ibn Baz, `Abdul-`Aziz, et al., *Abhath Hay'at Kibar Al-`Ulama'*, vol. 1 (Research of the Committee of Senior Clerics) (Cairo: Maktabat As-Sunnah, 1994), 447.

121. Ibid., 141.

122. Fatwa no. 3201, September 1, A.H. 1400, signed by members of the Permanent Committee; cited in ibid., 140.

123. Fatwa no. 1678, October 13, A.H. 1397, cited in Al-Wardani, *Fatawa*, 125.

124. Fatwa no. 1620, July 11 A.H. 1397, cited in ibid., 126–27.

125. Ibid, p. 127.

126. This according to a former U.S. ambassador in Saudi Arabia who met regularly with the crown prince.

127. Al-Wardani, *Fatawa*, 133.

128. Al-Wardani, *Ibn Baz*, 117–18.

129. Ibid., 118.

130. `Abdul-`Aziz Ibn Baz, *Majmu` Fatawa wa Maqalat Mutanwi`ah* (Collection of Fatwas and Miscellaneous Articles), vol. 2 (Riyad: Mu'assasat Ar-Risalah, A.H. 1421), 178.

131. See the text in *Majallat Al-Buhuth Al-Fiqhiyyah Al-Mu`asirah*, vol. 2, no. 6, 1990.

132. Ibid.

133. Tunisian writer Al-`Afif Al-Akhdar reported in 2003 on Al-Jazeera TV that he was banned from writing in the pro-Saudi newspaper *Al-Hayat* due to his attacks on Wahhabiyyah.

134. Cited in `Abdur-Rahman Al-Khayyir, *Ar-Rad `Ala Ibn Baz* (Response to Ibn Baz) (Damascus: Kutub Dhat Fa'idah, 1996), 10.

135. Text in *Fatawa Muhimmah li `Umum Al-Ummah* (Important Fatwas for the Entire Nation), cited in Ash-Shaykh Muhammad Shawqi Al-Haddad, *Al-Mawsu`ah Al-Wahhabiyyah wa-sh-Shi`a-l-Imamiyyah* (The Wahhabi Encyclopedia and Imamate Shi`ism) (Beirut: Dar Al-Ghadir, 1998), 17.

136. See the *New York Times*, May 28, 2003.

137. See *Al-Hayat*, March 21, 2004

138. Madawi Al-Rasheed, *A History of Saudi Arabia* (New York: Cambridge University Press, 2002), 39.

139. See Carl C. Brown, *International Politics and the Middle East: Old Rules, Dangerous Game* (Princeton: Princeton University Press, 1984).

140. Mohammed Almana, *Arabia Unified: A Portrait of Ibn Saud* (London: Hitchinson, 1980), 21.

141. Amin Rihani, *Muluk Al-`Arab* (The Kings of the Arabs), vol. 2 (Beirut: Sadir, 1929), 41.

142. `Abdul-`Aziz Al-Rashid, *Tarikh Al-Kuwayt* (History of Kuwait) (Beirut: Dar Maktabat Al-Hayat, 1971), 182.

143. Al-Rasheed, *A History of Saudi Arabia*, 41.
144. Nasir Al-Faraj, *Qiyam Al-`Arsh As-Su`udi* (The Establishment of the Saudi Throne) (London: Dar As-Safa, 1988), 35.
145. H. St. John Philby, *Arabian Highlands* (Ithaca: Cornell University Press and Middle East Institute, 1952).
146. G. Steinberg, "The Shiites in the Eastern Province of Saudi Arabia (Al-Ahasa'), 1913–1953," in *The Twelver Shia in Modern Times: Religious Culture and Political History*, eds. R. Brunner and W. Ende (Leiden: Brill, 2001), 243.
147. Al-Rasheed, *A History of Saudi Arabia*, 42.
148. Algar, *Wahhabism*, 42. The author told me that he obtained the figure from Aburish's book. See Said Aburish, *The Rise, Corruption and Coming Fall of the House of Saud* (New York: St. Martin's Press, 1994), 24.
149. Aburish, *The Rise, Corruption*, 24. As for much information in his book, Aburish does not cite any source for this figure.
150. As is known, Islam (and Muhammad personally) strongly urged the emancipation of slaves. In Islam per se, slavery was permitted in wartime and prohibited in peacetime. It was officially banned in 1962, but continued "unofficially" in royal households long after. See Bernard Lewis, *Race and Slavery in the Middle East: A Historical Inquiry* (New York: Oxford University Press, 1992).
151. This is quoted in Muhammad Jalal Kishk, *As-Sa`udiyyun wa-l-Hall Al-Islami: Masdar Ash-Shar`iyyah li-n-Nidham As-Sa`udi* (The Saudis and the Islamic Solution: The Source of Legitimacy for the Saudi Regime) (Cairo: Al-Matba`ah Al-Fanniyyah, 1981), 121. which is pro-Saudi source.
152. See Rihani, *Muluk*, 69.
153. John Glubb, *Arabian Adventures: 10 Years of Joyful Service* (London: Cassell, 1978). Also cited in Aburish, *The Rise, Corruption*, 24.
154. Glubb, *Arabian Adventures*.
155. Ibid., 69–70.
156. Ibid., 73.
157. Ibid., 74.
158. Al-Rasheed, *A History of Saudi Arabia*, 47.
159. The best treatment is in ibid., 49–59.
160. J. Habib, *Ibn Saud's Warriors of Islam: The Ikhwan of Najd and Their Role in the Creation of the Saudi Kingdom, 1910, 1930* (Leiden: Brill, 1978), 16.
161. Rihani, *Muluk*, 77.
162. As quoted in Fu'ad Ibrahim and Hamzah Al-Hasan, *Thuna'iyyat At-Ta'azzum fi-s-Su`udiyyah: Al-Hawiyyah, Ad-Din, Al-Qabilah* (The Duality of Crisis in Saudi Arabia: Identity, Religion, Tribe) (London: Qadaya Al-Khalij, 2003), 90.
163. Al-Katib, *Al-Fikr As-Siyasi Al-Wahhabi*, 124.
164. Surat Al-`Imran, Ayat 103; cited in Kishk, *As-Sa`udiyyun wa-l-Hall Al-Islami*, 555.
165. Rihani, *Muluk*, 95.
166. See Wahbah, *Jazirat Al-`Arab*, 227.

167. Sulayman Ibn Sahman, *Minhaj Ahl-Al-Haqq* (The Path of the People of Righteousness), (Ajman: Maktabat Al-Furqan, A.H. 1417), 90.

168. J. Kostiner, *The Making of Saudi Arabia, 1916–1936*, (London: Oxford University Press, 1993).

169. Al-Rasheed, *A History of Saudi Arabia*, 66.

170. Al-Katib, *Al-Fikr As-Siyasi Al-Wahhabi*, 135.

171. Wahbah, *Jazirat Al-`Arab*, 297.

172. Ibid., 297.

173. Ibid., 67.

174. Fahd Al-Qahtani, *Sira` Al-Ajnihah fi-l-`A'ilah As-Sa`udiyyah* (The Factional Struggle Within the Saudi Family) (London: Safa, 1988), 278.

175. Wahbah, *Jazirat Al-`Arab*, 309.

176. As cited in Tuwayjiri, *Li Surat Al-Layl Hatafa As-Sabah*, 466.

177. Khayr Ad-Din Az-Zirkili, *Shibh Al-Jazirah fi `Ahd Al-Malik `Abdul-`Aziz* (The Peninsula in the Era of King `Abdul-`Aziz) (Beirut: Dar Al-Qalam, 1970), 355–56.

178. H. St. John Philby, *Arabian Jubilee* (London: Hale, 1952), 111.

179. See Al-Qahtani, *Sira` Al-Ajnihah fi-l-`A'ilah As-Sa`udiyyah*.

180. Al-Rasheed, *A History of Saudi Arabia*, 75–76.

181. Jubran Shamiyyah, *Al Sa`ud: Madihum wa Mustaqbaluhum* (The House of Saud: Their Past and Future) (London: Riad El-Rayyes, 1986), 76. The title is misidentified in Al-Rasheed, *A History of Saudi Arabia*, as The House of Saud: Their Past and Present.

182. Al-Rasheed, *A History of Saudi Arabia*, 77.

183. Nasir As-Sa`id, *Tarikh Al-Sa`ud* (History of the House of Saud) (n.p.: n.d.). The author, a former schoolteacher/poet, uses information, innuendos, rumors, tales, and fabrications to construct his case against the House of Saud. Some of his theories are outright vulgar and prejudicial: his main theory for the corruption of the House of Saud has to do with his claim of the Jewish ancestry of the family.

184. Al-Qahtani, *Sira` Al-Ajnihah fi-l-`A'ilah As-Sa`udiyyah*, 38.

185. *New York Times*, November 30, 2001.

186. Lawrence Wright, "The Kingdom of Silence," *The New Yorker*, January 5, 2004, 53.

187. Text of his talk is in Kishk, *As-Sa`udiyyun wa-l-Hall Al-Islami*, 37–38.

188. Almana, *Arabia Unified*, 178.

189. Kishk, *As-Sa`udiyyun wa-l-Hall Al-Islami*, 72.

190. `Abdullah, *Al-`Ulama' Wa-l-`Arsh* 94.

191. Aburish, *The Rise, Corruption*, 35.

192. Ibid., 35.

193. Al-Rasheed, *A History of Saudi Arabia*, 93.

194. Ibid., 95.

195. See A. Brown, *Oil, God, and Gold: The Story of Aramco and the Saudi Kings* (Boston: Houghton Mifflin, 1999).

196. Ibid., 150.

197. The best source on internal dynamics of the royal family is Al-Qahtani, *Sira` Al-Ajnihah fi-l-`A'ilah As-Sa`udiyyah* 50.

198. Ibid., 49.

199. Aburish, *The Rise, Corruption*, 43.
200. Nadav Safran, *Saudi Arabia: The Ceaseless Quest for Security* (Cambridge, Mass.: Harvard University Press, 1985).
201. The best account is in F. Gregory Gause III, *Saudi-Yemeni Relations: Domestic Structures and Foreign Influence* (New York: Columbia University Press, 1990).
202. See a declassified CIA report posted at www.foia.cia.gov/ browse_docs.asp?doc_no=0000283499&title=UAR+-+YEMEN+-+SAUDI+ARABIA&abstract=&no_pages=0002&pub_date=3/15/1963&r elease_date=12/28/1999&keywords=SAUDI+ARABIA|NASIR|EGYPT|Y EMEN|UAR|PRINCE+FAYSAL&case_no=F-1997-00394&copy-right=0&release_dec=RIPPUB&classification=U&showPage=0001.
203. Al-Rasheed, *A History of Saudi Arabia*, 107.
204. Valuable information on the life and ideas of `Abdullah At-Tariqi, including interviews with his widow and advisors, were published in 2003 on the Arabic news Web site Elaph: www.elaph.com:9090/elaph/arabic/index.html.
205. Al-Rasheed, *A History of Saudi Arabia*, 111.
206. See his interview with Al-Jazeera, December 2000. See the transcripts at www.aljazeera.net/programs/century_witness/articles/2000/12/12-17-2.htm.
207. Al-Qahtani, *Sira` Al-Ajnihah fi-l-`A'ilah As-Sa`udiyyah* 88.
208. Al-Rasheed, *A History of Saudi Arabia*, 114.
209. Aburish, *The Rise, Corruption*, 45.
210. Al-Qahtani, *Sira` Al-Ajnihah fi-l-`A'ilah As-Sa`udiyyah*, 120–21.
211. Quoted in ibid., 143–44.
212. Aburish, *The Rise, Corruption*, 78.
213. The figures are in Al-Qahtani, *Sira` Al-Ajnihah fi-l-`A'ilah As-Sa`udiyyah*, 458.
214. Al-Rasheed, *A History of Saudi Arabia*, 127.
215. The classic account of Yamani is Jeffrey Robinson, *Yamani: The Inside Story* (London: Simon and Schuster, 1988). The author has read the Arabic translation published by the Saudi opposition in London.
216. See Fred Halliday, *Arabia Without Sultans* (London: Penguin, 1974), 415.
217. See Al-Qahtani, *Sira` Al-Ajnihah fi-l-`A'ilah As-Sa`udiyyah*, 474.
218. Mamoun Fandy, *Saudi Arabia and the Politics of Dissent* (New York: Palgrave, 1999).
219. Halliday, *Arabia Without Sultans*, 68.
220. Ibid., 68–69.
221. For a full treatment, see ibid.
222. May Yamani, "Cross Cultural Marriages within Islam: Ideals and Realities," in *Cross-Cultural Marriage*, eds. Rosemary Berger and R. Hill (Oxford: Berg, 1998).
223. Gause, *Saudi-Yemeni Relations*.
224. Details are well described in Shafiq Al-Hut, `Ishrun `Aman fi Munadhdhamat At-Tahrir, (Beirut: Dar Al-Istiqlal, 1986).
225. The full text is in *Umm Al-Qura*, March 7, 1969; cited in Jaffet Memorial Library, American University of Beirut, *Al-Watha'iq Al-`Arabiyyah* (Arab Political Documents) (Beirut: AUB, 1969), 199–200.

226. For an incisive and very well-informed treatment, see Ahmad Dallal, "The Origins and Objectives of Islamic Revivalist Thought, 1750–1850," *Journal of the American Oriental Society*, vol. 113, no. 3 (1993).

227. Al-Rasheed, *A History of Saudi Arabia*, 132.

228. Ibid.

229. Al-Qahtani, *Sira` Al-Ajnihah fi-l-`A'ilah As-Sa`udiyyah*, 147.

230. *Al-Muharrir*, April 8, 1975; cited in Al-Qahtani, *Sira` Al-Ajnihah fi-l-`A'ilah As-Sa`udiyyah*, 191.

231. Emile Nakhleh, *The United Sates and Saudi Arabia: A Policy Analysis* (Washington, D.C.: American Enterprise Institute, 1975).

232. Lacey, *The Kingdom*, 429.

233. Benoist Mechin, *Faycal: roi d'Arabie, 1906–1975* (Paris: A. Michel, 1975).

234. `Ali Ballut, article in *Ad-Dustur*, April 5, 1975.

235. See *As-Safir*, March 27 and 29, 1975.

236. *As-Safir*, March 29, 1975.

237. See the excellent treatment on this in Al-Qahtani, *Sira` Al-Ajnihah fi-l-`A'ilah As-Sa`udiyyah*, 168–69.

238. Ibid., 270.

239. Ibid., 271.

240. Ibid.

241. See Joseph A. Kechichian, "Saudi Arabia's Will to Power," in *Middle East Policy*, vol. VII, no. 2 (February 2000), 53.

242. See Graham, *Saudi Arabia Unveiled*, 22.

243. See Rif`at Sayyid Ahmad, *Rasa'il Juhayman Al-`Utaybi: Qa'id Al-Muqtahimin li-l-Masjid Al-Haram bi-Makka* (The Letters of Juhayman Al-`Utaybi: The Commanders of the Attackers of the Holy Mosque in Mecca) (Cairo: Madbuli, 1988), 11; and Al-Rasheed, *A History of Saudi Arabia*, 69.

244. See Mordechai Abir, *Saudi Arabia in the Oil Era: Regime and Elites, Conflict and Collaboration* (London: Croomhelm, 1988).

245. Ayman Al-Yassini, *Religion and State in the Kingdom of Saudi Arabia* (Boulder: Westview Press, 1985), 124.

246. Ahmad, *Rasa'il Juhayman Al-`Utaybi*, 21.

247. Ibid.

248. Ibid.

249. Full text is in ibid., 20–21.

250. See the account of the pro-Saudi Salim Al-Lawzi in *Al-Hawadith*, January 18, 1980.

251. From the text of a treatise by Al-`Utaybi, quoted in Ahmad, *Rasa'il Juhayman Al-`Utaybi*, 37.

252. Ibid., 38.

253. See ibid., 67.

254. Ibid., 69.

255. Lacey, *The Kingdom*, 435.

256. Ahmad, *Rasa'il Juhayman Al-`Utaybi*, 255.

257. Al-Rasheed, *A History of Saudi Arabia*, 147.

258. Ibid., 146.

259. A section of Nasir As-Sa`id's history of the House of Saud is devoted to the travails of King Fahd. See As-Sa`id, *Tarikh Al-Sa`ud.*

260. Woodward, *Veil.*

261. The letter is cited in Al-Qahtani, *Sira` Al-Ajnihah fi-l-`A'ilah As-Sa`udiyyah,* 213–14.

262. The text of the plan is on the following UN Web site: http://domino.un.org/UNISPAL.NSF/0/5fb09709f4050b8985256ced00739 0d8?OpenDocument.

263. Ibid.

264. Anthony H. Cordesman, *Strategic Stability in the Gulf: Key Economic and Demographic Trends* (Washington, D.C.: Center for Strategic and International Studies, 1998), 16.

265. The Consulting Center for Finance and Investment, Economic and Investment Research Division, *Saudi Budget 2002: Analysis and Implications* (Riyadh, Saudi Arabia: December 2001), 2.

266. Al-Rasheed, *A History of Saudi Arabia,* 150.

267. For a study of the council, see Fred Lawson, *Dialectical Integration of the Gulf Co-operation Council* (Abu Dhabi: Emirates Center for Strategic Research, 1997).

268. John Peterson, *The Gulf Cooperation Council: Search for Unity in a Dynamic Region* (Boulder, Col.: Westview Press, 1988), 106.

269. Al-Rasheed, *A History of Saudi Arabia,* 159.

270. Al-Qahtani, *Sira` Al-Ajnihah fi-l-`A'ilah As-Sa`udiyyah,* 217.

271. Ibid.

272. For an interesting profile of Prince Bandar, as he was trying to make a comeback after September 11 (by denigrating Arafat and the Palestinians), see (his friend) Elsa Walsh, "The Prince: How the Saudi Ambassador Became Washington's Indispensable Operator," *The New Yorker,* March 24, 2003.

273. He did so even in his early tract on the Islamic government. See Imam R. Khumayni, *Al-Hukumah Al-Islamiyyah* (Beirut: Dar At-Tali`ah, 1979).

274. See the Iranian published set of assembled shredded documents. See Danishjuyan-I Musalman-I Payraw-i Khatt-i Imam, *Asnad-I lanah-I jasusi-I Amrika* (Documents from the U.S. Espionage Den), vol. 39 (Tehran: Danishjuyan-i Musalman-i Payraw-i Khatt-i Imam, 1985).

275. Woodward, *Veil.*

276. The text is published in a book by a former media star of Saddam's government who is now a close media ally of the U.S. occupation force in Baghdad. See Sa`d Al-Bazzaz,, *Harb Talid Ukhra: At-Tarikh As-Sirri li-Harb Al-Khalij* (A War That Begot Another War: The Secret History of the Gulf War) (Amman: Al-Ahliyyah, 1992), 65–68.

277. Ibid., 66–67.

278. See Al-Qahtani, *Sira` Al-Ajnihah fi-l-`A'ilah As-Sa`udiyyah,* 301.

279. As quoted in the official quasi-biography (which contains more information on Saudi infrastructure than on the life of Fahd): Fouad Al-Farsy *Custodian of the Two Holy Mosques, King Fahd Bin Abdul Aziz* (Channel Islands: Knight Communications, 2001), 53.

280. For biographical information and references to his thought, see Fandy, *Saudi Arabia and the Politics of Dissent*, 61–87.

281. See, for example, Safar Al-Hawali, *Wa`d Kissinger wa-l-Ahdaf Al-Amirkiyyah fi-l-Khalij* (The Promise of Kissinger and the American Goals in the Gulf) (Dallas: Mu'assasat Al-Kitab Al-Islami, 1991).

282. Al-Rasheed, *A History of Saudi Arabia*, 165–66.

283. Fandy, *Saudi Arabia and the Politics of Dissent*, 63.

284. See the treatment in Fandy, *Saudi Arabia and the Politics of Dissent*, 89–113.

285. These accounts are based on written descriptions written by the activists themselves and smuggled outside of the kingdom; they were read by the author.

286. See Al-Rasheed, *A History of Saudi Arabia*, 168–69.

287. Ibid., 169.

288. See Fandy, *Saudi Arabia and the Politics of Dissent*, 50–54.

289. See the interview with Prince Sultan, *Al-Hawadith*, March 6, 1987.

290. See the interview with Prince Nayif, *Al-Hawadith*, March 6, 1987.

291. Al-Rasheed, *A History of Saudi Arabia*, 171.

292. From an interview with *Rose Al-Yusuf*, August 11, 1975.

293. Al-Farsy, *Custodian of the Two Holy Mosques*, 181.

294. See the composition breakdown in Fandy, *Saudi Arabia and the Politics of Dissent*, 40.

295. Al-Rasheed, *A History of Saudi Arabia*, 174.

296. Al-Farsy, *Custodian of the Two Holy Mosques*, 182.

297. See the discussion in Al-Katib, *Al-Fikr As-Siyasi Al-Wahhabi*, 160–61.

298. See *Forbes* magazine, April 2003.

299. This estimate is generally agreed upon in Western press reports. See the information at www.saudhouse.com/how_much.htm.

300. See the information at
www.saudhouse.com/abdul_aziz_bin_fahd.htm.

301. Al-Rasheed, *A History of Saudi Arabia*, 173.

302. See Al-Katib, *Al-Fikr As-Siyasi Al-Wahhabi*, 161.

303. See ibid., 175.

304. As quoted in ibid.

305. Bob Woodward, *The Commanders*, (New York: Simon and Schuster, 1991).

306. For more on the visit, see *Al-Hayat*, September 4, 2003.

307. As cited in *Al-Quds Al-`Arabi*, September 4, 2003.

308. See the report in *Ash-Sharq Al-Awsat*, September 2, 2003.

309. See the *New York Times*, March 20, 2004.

310. See the products MEMRI, the pro-Israeli translation outfit based in Washington, D.C., which specializes in dishing out an unending supply of vulgar, silly, and stupid statements dug out from the Arabic and Persian press. See, for example, *Preliminary Overview: Saudi Arabia's Education System*, Special Report no. 12, December 2002. It should be noted that "retired" officials from the Israeli intelligence agency, the Mossad, founded this MEMRI, a favorite of *New York Times* reporters and columnists. See the investigate article "Selective MEMRI," *Guardian* (London), August 12, 2002.

311. Simon Henderson, Simon, *After King Fahd: Succession in Saudi Arabia* (Washington, D.C.: Washington Institute for Near East Policy, 1994), 28.
312. Ibid.
313. A former U.S. ambassador in Saudi Arabia told this to me.
314. *Der Spiegel*, March 8, 2004.
315. See Nimrod Raphaeli "Saudi Arabia: A Brief Guide to Its Politics and Problems," *MERIA Journal*, vol.. 7, no. 3 (September 2003).
316. Ibid.
317. Ibid.
318. *Qu'an*, Surat Az-Zalzalah.
319. *Qur'an*, 3:110.
320. Fandy, *Saudi Arabia and the Politics of Dissent*, 27.
321. Muslim World League, *Rabitat Al-`Alam Al-Islami* (Muslim World League) (Jiddah: Muslim World League, 1987), 163.
322. Ibid.
323. Ibid., 55.
324. Ibid., 69.
325. Ibid.
326. Ibid.
327. Ibid., 68–70.
328. See the new report at www.abc.net.au/am/content/2003/s920069.htm.
329. See the annual report of Al-Haramain Foundation for the year A.H. 1422.
330. See the works of Ihsan Dhahir, such as *Ash-Shi`ah wa Ahl-Al-Abayt* (The Shi`ites and Ahl Al-Bayt) (Lahore: Idarat Tarjuman As-Sunnah).
331. Leila Ahmed, *Women and Gender in Islam* (New Haven: Yale University Press, 1993).
332. See Salih Al-Wardani, *Ibn Baz: Faqih Al Su`ud* (Ibn Baz: The Theologian of the House of Saud) (Cairo: Dar Husam, 1998).
333. The ban on female driving was only officially codified into religious law in 1992, after the attempt by some women to defy the ban in Riyadh.
334. From a fatwa by Bin Baz, www.uh.edu/campus/msa/articles/fatawawom/know.html#seeking, January 7, 2002.
335. "Getting Their Cards," *The Economist*, January 3, 2002.
336. *2003 CIA World Factbook*, www.cia.gov/cia/publications/factbook/geos/sa.html.
337. `Abdul-Muta'ali Al-Jabri, *Al-Mar'ah Fi-t-Tasawwur Al-Islami* (Women in the Islamic Perspective) (n.p.: n.d.).
338. See the informative section in Mona Al-Monajjed *Women in Saudi Arabia Today* (New York: St. Martin's Press, 1997), 59–80.
339. Ibid., 62.
340. Ibid., 65.
341. Baqir Salman An-Najjar, *Al-Mar'ah fi-l-Khalij Al-`Arabi wa Tahawwulat Al-Hadathah Al-`Asirah* (Women in the Arab Gulf and the Changes of a Difficult Modernity) (Beirut: Al-Markaz Ath-Thaqafi Al-`Arabi, 2000), 81–83.
342. Ahmad Jamal Dhahir, *Al-Mar'ah fi Duwal Al-Khalij Al-`Arabi: Dirasah Maydaniyyah* (Women in the Arab Gulf States: An Empirical Study) (Kuwait: Dhat As-Salasil, 1983), 140.

343. Clifford Geertz, *Islam Observed: Religious Development In Morocca and Indonesia* (Chicago: University of Chicago Press, 1968).

344. Dhahir, *Al-Mar'ah fi Duwal Al-Khalij Al-`Arabi*, 236.

345. Ibid., 106.

346. Ibid., 106.

347. As cited in Al-Monajjed, *Women in Saudi Arabia Today*, 81.

348. Dhahir, *Al-Mar'ah fi Duwal Al-Khalij Al-`Arabi*, 168.

349. Cited in Al-Monajjed, *Women in Saudi Arabia Today*, 82.

350. "Putting Saudi Women to Work," *The Economist*, September 24, 1998.

351. Dhahir, *Al-Mar'ah fi Duwal Al-Khalij Al-`Arabi*, 168.

352. Cited in W. Powell, *Saudi Arabia and Its Royal Family* (Secaucus, N.J.: Lyle Stuart, 1982), 140.

353. Eleanor Abdella Doumato, "Women and Work in Saudi Arabia: How Flexible Are Islamic Margins?" *The Middle East Journal*, vol. 53, no. 4 (Autumn 1999), 569.

354. Amnesty International Public Document, AI Index MDE 23/036/2000, News Service no. 84, May 10, 2000.

355. Amnesty International, *Women in Saudi Arabia*, extracted from www.amnesty-usa.org/countries/saudi_arabia/women/index.html.

356. See Dhahir, *Al-Mar'ah fi Duwal Al-Khalij Al-`Arabi*, p. 194.

357. Ibid.

358. See http://www.hipakistan.com/en/detail.php?newsId=en50671&F_catID=&f_type=source.

359. The most comprehensive sketch is in Fandy, *Saudi Arabia and the Politics of Dissent*, 43–60.

360. See `Abd-un-Nabi Al-`Akri (the Engineer), *At-Tandhimat Al-Yasariyyah fi-l-Jazirah wa-l-Khalij Al-`Arabi* (Left-wing Organizations in Arabia and the Arabian Gulf) (Beirut: Dar Al-Kunuz Al-Adabiyyah, 2003), 39.

361. The reference here is to various issues of the mouthpiece of the Saudi Communist Party, *Tariq Al-Kadihin.* See, for example, issues 34 (February 1987) and 40 (February 1988).

362. See the mouthpiece of the Union of Workers in Saudi Arabia, *Sawt Al-`Ummal*, February 1987.

363. See Amnesty International report at www.amnesty.org/ailib/intcam/tunion/1998/sarabia.htm.

364. See Hamzah Al-Hasan, "`Alaqat Shi`at As-Su`udiyyah Al-Kharijiyyah: Madhhabiyyan wa Siyasiyyan" (The External Relations of the Saudi Shi`ites: Confessionally, and Politically), Al-Jazeera.net, May 31, 2003, at www.amnesty.org/ailib/intcam/tunion/1998/sarabia.htm.

365. Fandy, *Saudi Arabia and the Politics of Dissent*, 45.

366. See ibid., ch. 4.

367. Al-Rasheed, *A History of Saudi Arabia*, 176.

368. Fandy, *Saudi Arabia and the Politics of Dissent*, 122.

369. Ibid., 154.

370. Al-Rasheed, *A History of Saudi Arabia*, 177.

371. The collection of the political literature of the group is CDLR, *Madha Taqulu Lajnat ad-Difa`an Al-Huquq Ash-Shar`iyyah fi-l-Jazirah Al-*

    `Arabiyyah` (What Does the CDLR in the Arabian Peninsula Have to Say) (London: Ad-Dar Ash-Shar`iyyah, 1994), 14–18.

372. Ibid.

373. See the English/Arabic Web site at www.cdlr.net/.

374. Muhammad Al-Mas`ari, *Al-Adillah Al-Qat`iyyah `Ala `Adam Shar`iyyat Ad-Dawla-s-Sa`udiyyah* (The Decisive Proofs on the Illegality [from the Islamic point of view] of the Saudi State) (London: CDLR, 2001).

375. Fandy, *Saudi Arabia and the Politics of Dissent*, 150.

376. See the English/Arabic Web site at www.yaislah.org/.

377. See Fandy, *Saudi Arabia and the Politics of Dissent*, 172–73.

378. See www.yaislah.org/documents/Stats.htm.

379. Ibid.

380. See Fandy, *Saudi Arabia and the Politics of Dissent*, 167.

381. See Fandy, *Saudi Arabia and the Politics of Dissent*, 168.

382. See *Al-Islah*, no. 161, May 17, 1999.

383. Fandy, *Saudi Arabia and the Politics of Dissent*, 199.

384. Hasan As-Saffar, *At-Ta`addudiyyah wa-l-Huriyyah fi-l-Islam* (Pluralism and Liberty in Islam) (Beirut: Dar Al-Bayan Al-`Arabi, 1990).

385. Fandy, *Saudi Arabia and the Politics of Dissent*, 200.

386. The reference here is to the author's collection of the issues of *Al-Jazirah Al-`Arabiyyah* from 1991 to 1994.

387. Fandy, *Saudi Arabia and the Politics of Dissent*, 200.

388. As`ad AbuKhalil, *Bin Laden, Islam, and America's New "War on Terrorism,"* (New York: Seven Stories Press, 2002).

389. See his statement in *Al-Hayat*, September 8, 2003.

390. U.S. Department of State, *Country Reports on Human Rights Practices, 2002 Saudi Arabia* (Washington, D.C.: U.S. Department of State, Bureau of Democracy, Human Rights, and Labor, March 2003), at www.state.gov/g/drl/rls/hrrpt/2002/18288.htm.

391. Ibid., Libya, at www.state.gov/g/drl/rls/hrrpt/2001/nea/8273.htm.

392. Minnesota Lawyers International Human Rights Committee, *Shame in the House of Saud: Contempt for Human Rights in the Kingdom of Saudi Arabia* (Minneapolis, Minn.: Minnesota Lawyers International Human Rights Committee, 1992), vii.

393. Ibid.

394. Amnesty International, *Saudi Arabia: A Secret State of Suffering* (New York: Amnesty International, January 23, 2000), 16.

395. Amnesty International, *Report 2003* (New York: Amnesty International, 2003), 213.

396. Minnesota Lawyers International Human Rights Committee, *Shame in the House of Saud*, 20.

397. See ibid.

398. Amnesty International, *Saudi Arabia: A Secret*, 15.

399. Ibid.

400. Al-Lajnah Ad-Duwaliyyah Li-d-Difa` `An Huquq Al-Insan fi-l-Khalij wa-l-Jazira-l-`Arabiyyah, *Huquq Al-Insan fi-l-Mamlaka-l-`Arabiyya-s-Sa`udiyyah* (Human Rights in the Kingdom of Saudi Arabia), (n.p.: -Lajnah

Ad-Duwaliyyah Li-d-Difa` `An Huquq Al-Insan fi-l-Khalij wa-l-Jazira-l-`Arabiyyah, 1989), 87.

401. Amnesty International, *Saudi Arabia: Behind Closed Doors: Unfair Trials in Saudi Arabia* (New York: Amnesty International, 1997), 22.

402. Amnesty International, *Saudi Arabia: An Upsurge in Public Executions* (New York: Amnesty International, May 1993).

403. Amnesty International, *Saudi Arabia: Behind Closed Doors*, 22.

404. Ibid.

405. Al-Lajnah Ad-Duwaliyyah Li-d-Difa` `An Huquq Al-Insan fi-l-Khalij wa-l-Jazira-l-`Arabiyyah, *Huquq Al-Insan fi-l-Mamlaka-l-`Arabiyya-s-Sa`udiyyah* 145.

406. Minnesota Lawyers International Human Rights Committee, *Shame in the House of Saud*, 24.

407. Ibid., 27.

408. Ibid.

409. Amnesty International, *Saudi Arabia: Torture, Detention, and Arbitrary Arrests* (New York: Amnesty International, 1990), 1.

410. Amnesty International, *Report 2003*, 215.

411. Minnesota Lawyers International Human Rights Committee, *Shame in the House of Saud*, 41–42.

412. As quoted in Muhammad An-Nayrab, *Usul Al-`Alaqat As-Sa`udiyyah Al-Amirkiyyah* (The Origins of U.S.-Saudi Relations) (Cairo: Madbuli, 1994), 45.

413. Ibid., 158.

414. Ibid., 197.

415. Lacey, *The Kingdom*, 257.

416. The author was told this by an American who met with the crown prince regularly.

417. The text is in As-Sa`id, *Tarikh Al-Sa`ud*, 868.

418. See the interview in *Life*, May 31, 1943; cited in An-Nayrab, *Usul Al-`Alaqat As-Sa`udiyyah Al-Amirkiyyah*, 202–03.

419. As quoted in Lacey, *The Kingdom*, 258.

420. See Henry Kissinger, *White House Years* (New York: Little, Brown, 1979).

421. As quoted in Lacey, *The Kingdom*, 271.

422. An-Nayrab, *Usul Al-`Alaqat As-Sa`udiyyah Al-Amirkiyyah*, 207.

423. Cited in ibid., 272.

424. See Nathan Citino, *From Arab Nationalism to OPEC: Eisenhower, King Sa`ud and the Making of U.S.-Saudi Relations* (Bloomington, Ind.: Indiana University Press, 2002).

425. On the newly discovered anti-Semitic entries in Truman's diary, see www.jewishsf.com/bk030718/us02.shtml.

426. Harry S Truman, *Public Papers of the Presidents of the United States, Containing the Public Messages, Speeches, and Statements of the President, 1946, January 1 to December 31, 1946* (Washington, D.C.: Government Printing Office, 1962), 467–69.

427. See Evan M. Wilson, *Decision on Palestine: How the U.S. Came to Recgonize Israel* (Stanford, Calif.: Hoover Institution Press, Stanford University, 1979).

428. Lacey, *The Kingdom*, 289.

429. See the fawning account of King Saud by Alfred M. Lilienthal, "The King (Saud of Saudi Arabia) and I: Eyewitness to History," *The Washington Report on Middle East Affairs*, March 1995, 31–32.

430. Lacey, *The Kingdom*, 307.

431. See J. B. Kelly, *Arabia, the Gulf, and the West* (New York: Basic Books, 1980).

432. Ibid., 31.

433. See Joel Beinin, *Was the Red Flag Flying There? Marxist Politics and the Arab-Israeli Conflict in Egypt and Israel, 1948–1965* (Berkeley: University of California Press, 1990).

434. Se Muhyi-d-Din, Khalid, *Wa-l-An Atakallam* (Cairo: Markaz Al-Ahram li-t-Tarjamah wa-n-Nashr, 1992).

435. See the memoirs of former CIA Middle East expert Archibald Roosevelt, *For Lust of Knowing: Memoirs of an Intelligence Officer* (Boston: Little, Brown, 1988).

436. Ibid.

437. Lacey, *The Kingdom*, 315.

438. For the trial of Qulaylat and his associates, see Muhsin Salim, *Murafa`at Al-Ustadh Muhsin Salim amama Majlis Al-`Adl fi Qadiyyat Ightiyal Kamil Muruwwah* (The Defense Statement of Mr. Muhsin Salim Before the Council of Justice in the Case of the Assassination of Kamil Muruwwah) (Beirut: Maktab Muhsin Salim, 1999).

439. See Mervat Hatem, "The Paradoxes of State Feminism in Egypt," in *Women and Politics Worldwide*, eds. Barbara Nelson and N. Chowdhury (New Haven, Conn.: Yale University Press, 1994).

440. For this, see Fouad Ajami, *The Arab Predicament: Arab Political Thought and Practice Since 1967*, (New York: Cambridge University Press, 1981).

441. *New York Times*, May 12, 1977; cited in Steven Emerson, *The American House of Saud: The Secret Petrodollar Connection*,:(NY: F. Watts, 1985), 412. It should be noted that Emerson studies Saudi influence through the same prism that hateful anti-Semites study Jewish "influence" and "conspiracies."

442. Ibid., 407.

443. www.saudiembassy.net/gov_profile/bio_bandar.html.

444. The author discusses such matters in AbuKhalil, *Bin Laden, Islam.*

445. See the transcript of the interview at more.abcnews.go.com/sections/wnt/dailynews/saudi020314.html.

446. From a text of a speech by Prince Turki at Georgetown University in 2002. For the text of the speech, see www.ccasonline.org/publicaffairs/turki_02032002.html.

447. See *The Economist*, September 13, 2001.

448. See the PBS interview with Prince Bandar at www.ccasonline.org/publicaffairs/turki_02032002.html.

449. See the sensational and undocumented Gerald Posner, *Why America Slept: The Failure to Prevent 9/11*, (New York: Random House, 2003).

450. See George Mitchell and William S. Cohen, *Men of Zeal: A Candid Inside Story of the Iran-Contra Hearings* (New York: Viking, 1988).

451. See Woodward, *Veil.*

452. Walsh, "The Prince."

453. Interviewed by Eric Rouleau. See Eric Rouleau, "Trouble in the Kingdom," *Foreign Affairs*, vol. 81, no. 4 (July/August 2002), 77.

454. See the full account, and the account of `Abdullah's recounting, in F. Gregory Gause III, "Saudi Perceptions of the U.S. Since 9-11" (unpublished paper, October 2002).

455. See ibid. and Eric Rouleau, "Trouble in the Kingdom."

456. See Powell's speech on the initiative at www.state.gov/r/pa/prs/ps/2002/15923.htm.

457. See the interview in *Al-Quds Al-`Arabi*, December 14–15, 2002.

458. See Gause, "Saudi Perceptions."

459. See the article by Hamzah Al-Hasan in *Al-Quds Al-`Arabi*, December 11, 2002, 13.

460. Ibid.

461. James Zogby, *What Arabs Think: Values, Beliefs, and Concerns* (Utica: Zogby International, September 2002), 8.

462. Ibid., 20.

463. Ibid., 34.

464. Ibid., 49.

465. Ibid., 61.

466. Ibid.

467. Zogby International, *The Ten Nation Impressions of America Poll* (Utica: Zogby International, unpublished, April 2002), 18. The author is grateful to John Zogby for sharing the results of his study.

468. Ibid., 16.

469. Ibid., 19.

470. Ibid., 22.

471. Ibid.

472. Ibid., 25.

473. Eric Rouleau, "Trouble in the Kingdom," 76.

474. See *Al-Quds Al-`Arabi*, April 20–21, 2002.

475. The most detailed account is in Walsh, "The Prince."

476. Gause, F. G IIL, "Saudi…"

477. See "Teaming Up Again? The U.S. and Saudia Arabia are working together to build an antiterrorist task force despite tensions over the 9/11 report," *Time*, September 1, 2003.

478. See the official statement by Prince Saud at www.saudinf.com/main/y5984.htm.

479. Al-Jubayr was a classmate of the author's at Georgetown University. He served as a propagandist for the Saudi royal family even back then.

480. See *St. Petersburg Times*, May 8, 2002.

481. *New York Post*, May 1, 2002.

482. Ibid.

483. The best example is Emerson *The American House of Saud*. Emerson is the same "terrorism expert" who asserted on international TV that Muslims were behind the Oklahoma City bombing.

484. For the text of Kerry's speech, see www.johnkerry.com/pressroom/speeches/spc_2003_1203.html.

485. See *San Francisco Chronicle*, October 29, 2003, A 4.

486. See "Bush advisors cashed in on Saudi gravy train," *Boston Herald*, December 11, 2001. The author is indebted to his friend Tara Lynn Schendel for her assistance in locating data on the Carlyle Group.

487. See "Meet the Carlyle Group," *Guardian* (London), October 31, 2001.

488. See "Carlyle's Way," *Red Herring*, January 8, 2002.

489. See his statement in *Al-Hayat*, October 23, 2003.

490. Ibid.

491. Ibid.

492. For his statements, see *Al-Hayat*, October 16, 2003.

493. *Arab Times*, no. 415, 2003, 10.

494. See *Gulf News*, December 1, 2003.

495. Eric Laurent, *La guerre des Bush: Les secrets inavouables d'un conflit* (Paris: Plon, 2003).

496. Michael Moore, *Dude, Where's My Country?* (New York: Warner, 2003).

497. See Thomas Friedman, "The Houses of Bush and Sharon," *International Herald Tribune*, November 14, 2003.

498. See "Some 100 leading Saudi Arabians have signed a petition urging the government to speed up political reform," at news.bbc.co.uk/2/hi/middle_east/3344655.stm.

499. See *Al-Quds Al-`Arabi*, March 23, 2004.

500. Michael Doran gets carried away in his emphasis on the conflict between Crown Prince `Abdullah and Prince Nayif. See Michael Scott Doran, "The Saudi Paradox," *Foreign Affairs*, January–February 2004.

About the Author

As'ad AbuKhalil was born in Tyre, Lebanon. He received his B.A. and M.A. in political science from the American University of Beirut, and his Ph.D. in comparative politics from Georgetown University. AbuKhalil has taught at Georgetown, George Washington University, Tufts University, Colorado College, and Randolph-Macon Women's College. He is the author of *Historical Dictionary of Lebanon* (Scarecrow Press, 1988) and *Bin Ladin, Islam, and America's New "War on Terrorism"* (Seven Stories, 2002). His articles on Middle East politics and society have appeared in English, German, Spanish, and Arabic. He is professor of political science at California State University, Stanislaus, and visiting professor at the Center for Middle Eastern Studies at the University of California at Berkeley. You can visit As`ad AbuKhalil's Web page at angryarab.blogspot.com.

Index